Women, Men, and Money

Women, Men & Money

The Four Keys for Using Money to Nourish Your
Relationship, Bankbook, and Soul

William Francis Devine, Jr.

Harmony Books / New York

To Nancy

Published by Harmony Books, a division of Crown Publishers, Inc., 201 East 50th Street, New York, New York 10022. Member of the Crown Publishing Group.

Random House, Inc. New York, Toronto, London, Sydney, Auckland
http://www.randomhouse.com/

HARMONY and colophon are trademarks of Crown Publishers, Inc.

Printed in the United States of America

Design by Debbie Glasserman

Library of Congress Cataloging-in-Publication Data
Devine, William Francis.
    Women, men, and money : the four keys for using money to
    nourish your relationship, bankbook, and soul / by William
    Francis Devine, Jr.—1st ed.
    Includes index.
    1. Married people—Finance, Personal. 2. Finance, Personal.
I. Title.
HG179.D495 1998
332.024—dc21   97-21875

    ISBN 0-517-70764-0

10 9 8 7 6 5 4 3 2 1
First Edition

Author's Note

The ideas presented herein are the direct result of my day-to-day work with clients. Consequently, this book includes numerous anecdotes involving actual transactions and actual cases of people trying to make money work for them.

As an attorney I am obligated to protect the interests of my clients and to respect the interests of others with whom I work. Some anecdotes, therefore, have been altered in a way that preserves the participants' right to privacy without distorting the essential truth of their experience.

Contents

••

Acknowledgments

I am deeply grateful to the following people for their contributions to this book.

Many clients have shared with me significant portions of their experience with money. I salute them because such generosity takes a certain type of courage, and I thank them, because much of what follows is what we learned together.

Vimala Rodgers generously devoted an enormous amount of time and energy to helping me cradle the vision of this book, especially during its very early stages.

Dan and Jennifer Anderson, Grace Stratos Arias, Andy Bechtolsheim, Luis and Nancy Belmonte, Pam Bunce, Bill and Marguerite Devine, Bobbe and Glenn George, Dee and Ed Jordan, Lynn and Randy Knox, and David and Lynne Madison graced me with unflagging, inspiring support as I wrote. Jay Kajimura, Dusty LaHaye, Ben Mancini, and Michelle Rubin read the earliest versions of the manuscript and offered helpful suggestions.

Barbara Moulton of the Moulton Agency was brilliant in helping me organize my ideas and in representing me.

I am indebted to Leslie Meredith at Harmony Books for wanting to publish this book. She and Sherri Rifkin made invaluable contributions to it with their deft editorial remarks and their splendid energy. Brian Belfiglio, Joanna Burgess, and Andrew Stuart at Harmony also provided valuable guidance and spirited helpfulness. Donna Ryan enhanced the text with her skillful copyediting. Whitney Cookman designed an excellent jacket.

Amanda Evans Devine delivered an impeccable performance as the manuscript's circulating manager.

Most of all, I wish to thank Nancy Evans Devine, my wife. Her wisdom, love, and eloquent heart lift my writing and my life.

Let me not to the marriage of true minds
Admit impediments; love is not love
Which alters when it alteration finds
Or bends with the remover to remove.
O, no, it is an ever-fixed mark
That looks on tempests and is never shaken;
It is the star to every wand'ring bark,
Whose worth's unknown, although his height be taken.
Love's not Time's fool, though rosy lips and cheeks
Within his bending sickle's compass come;
Love alters not with his brief hours and weeks,
But bears it out even to the edge of doom.
  If this be error, and upon me proved,
  I never writ, nor no man ever loved.

—William Shakespeare

Introduction

Years ago I was approached by an established businessman about launching a company together. The opportunity was not a perfect one for me, but because of the income and experience it appeared to present, I was willing to proceed.

As we discussed hiring plans one day, I mentioned, "Nancy pointed out—"

"Your wife has never started a company," the businessman broke in, "so her opinion doesn't count. She's a nice person, but on these issues, treat her like she's stupid."

Stunned by the suggestion that I compromise my marriage for money, and enraged at hearing my wife called stupid, I gathered myself on my end of the telephone line and killed the deal.

Since that episode I have found work that fits me impeccably, thanks in no small part to Nancy's support and talented assistance. This work satisfies me more than launching that company ever could have, and it serves people as well as I can currently conceive. It leaves me time to support and assist Nancy with her writing. It is wonderfully lucrative.

Only recently have I seen that, in killing that deal, I was not only being faithful to my promise to love Nancy but also making good on my promise as a human being. As we grow together, I'm increasingly amazed at the value of being true to my promise.

OUR RETURN ON MONEY

As an attorney who arranges deals on single-family houses, I advise a lot of couples. Because houses cost so much, my clients frequently confront difficult decisions involving money. When this happens, I set forth for the couple the options as I see them, then wait for the question that typically follows: "Any advice?"

"You need to take care of your relationship, your bankbook, and your soul," I remind them.

"Are you saying we should be considerate of the buyers and not ask for too much?" The dollars have a grip on their minds.

"Not at all. Ask for exactly what you want. Their happiness is not your responsibility."

"Well, then, do you mean we should get as much as we can from the deal, then make sure to spend it on what's important to us?"

"No. If you go at it that way, you'll spend too much time struggling for the dollars. You have to be talented enough to use money to acquire more than mere dollars."

"I'm not sure we have the talent to do that."

"I'm certain that you do."

Silence often ensues. Finally, their attention not completely devoured by the cash, they ask, "So what exactly do you recommend we do?"

This book is what I recommend they do. For fifteen years I have helped people handle money. I have worked with individuals on the Forbes 400 list as well as people whose income hovers near the poverty line. I have advised people who hoped to be rich and folks who didn't care about that; couples who were in sync and partners who seemed intent on hurting each other; some who presumed they were financial wizards and others who assumed they knew nothing.

I have counseled Fortune 500 companies and global financial institutions on transactions involving large sums of pension and corporate funds. I have worked on both a $100 million real estate deal and a $20 parking ticket.

Having examined all these experiences closely, I conclude that people who use money best negotiate their lives with four basic principles in mind and secure for themselves not only significant financial success but also intimacy with their mates and a profound peace of mind. Accordingly, I recommend to my clients that they practice the four fundamentals of money.

Women, Men, and Money explains the four fundamentals for using money to nourish your relationship, your bankbook, and your soul. It offers numerous examples and practices that show you and your partner how to lift yourselves over the inevitable conflicts money will cause you, how to generate the funds to support yourselves, and how to deepen the connection between the two of you as you go together through life.

As rich as the return from money can be, many people never experience it. Using money well can make us wealthy beyond measure, yet we commonly find ourselves settling for a yield on our dollars that is actually quite paltry. Why is this?

In large part, the answer is that most of the financial discussions that surround us today are unconscious ones that totally ignore the full spectrum of money's purposes and rewards. An 8 percent mortgage is nice, many say, but if I could get one at $7^7/8$ percent, I'd really be doing well. If you would cut your own hair, others advise, you could save $200 a year. To raise

$10,000, you must save $150 a month without deviation for about five years, some tell you, which means you'd better stay on that job. That woman has no track record as an entrepreneur, experts declare, so she could not possibly start a company.

This overflow of relentlessly linear thinking creates a mindset from which little is possible in life. Money, the thinking goes, couldn't possibly work so well for me that it would yield self-esteem, intimacy, and a meaningful connection to customers in addition to material support. I'm not talented enough to reap that rich a reward. My efforts won't really improve my lot. Money doesn't really work that way. If I can just pay the bills from now until the end, I'll settle for that.

Financial discussions, with our partners or with others, are reduced to contests in which one side will lose. Changing our work, a move that could radically enhance both our lives and our finances, becomes a pipe dream full of unthinkable risk. When the boss makes a demand or the rent is overdue, rapport between partners takes second place to finance, because love is assumed to have no cash value.

When we do not aim for an expansive return from money, we typically find ourselves out of sync with those we love, worrying chronically over surprisingly trivial sums, and living lives of silent regret. We struggle, live fearfully, and live small.

You and your partner can do better than this. You need not settle for so meager a standard of living. You can step toward a life worthy of your talents, spirit, and vision by employing the principles outlined in the pages ahead.

I have worked with couples making investments, couples changing jobs and embracing great career risk, and couples with all manner of deals to negotiate. I have seen couples at the brink of emotional and financial bankruptcy engineer inspiring reversals of fortune. I have seen couples earn mutual admiration, self-respect, and enormous wealth from intelligently embracing huge financial risks that rip other couples apart or frighten them away. I have seen couples calmly sidestep moves that would have damaged their relationship deeply and cost them tens of thousands of dollars.

What I know is that, regardless of your net worth, your job title, or how talented you think you are, you and your partner can earn, spend, invest, negotiate, and communicate about money in a way that will support a healthy life and supply you with plenty of cash. One couple with no extensive business experience used these principles to build a software firm that netted them a tremendous buy-out check and a life together free of normal job constraints. A couple who never fancied themselves negotiators used these principles to earn $30,000 extra on the sale of their house and to turn what looked initially like a stressful, expensive deal into a simple, profitable experience. Many people transform their finances, enhance their relationship, and find a sense of unexpected freedom and momentum when they realize, thanks to these fundamentals, that they can forgo financial maneuvers they once assumed were compulsory.

My experience, and the experience of many others I have observed over the years, is that this rich, multifaceted return from money is our birthright as human beings. You and your partner need not be overwhelmed by the magnitude of the transaction. The steps for making the deal are few and straightforward. How can this be? The experience is not unlike learning to ski an intimidating mountainside.

Your first impression is that you have a lot of difficult things to do. As you practice, however, you realize that there's less to do than you thought. In fact, as you master the slope, you realize that an inspiring, satisfying run is a function of making sure not to do too much. Other influences much more powerful than you—gravity and the human spirit, to name two—will do most of the work if you let them.

MY STORY WITH MONEY

How do I know so much about money? My understanding has emerged over time. Three experiences in particular have been pivotal to my development.

Several years after starting my own real estate practice, I worked on a short-term assignment for a Wall Street investment house. I took the assignment quite eagerly, thinking that I would learn a lot from the Harvard-Stanford-Yale types who ran the firm.

This indeed turned out to be the case, but not in the way I expected. The full story is presented in Chapter 4. In short, the man running the project, who spent a considerable portion of each day reminding people of his impressive title and his Ivy League pedigree, thoroughly mishandled $250,000 of the client's funds, thereby embarrassing himself, angering his bosses, and upsetting the client.

The experience confirmed a theory I had been testing for several years. Thereafter, it became a permanent part of my thinking: people you expect to know how to handle dollar bills often don't.

My next defining money experience was a course in wealth and financial planning that Nancy and I took shortly after we married. The substance of the course was the traditional stuff of personal finance: dollar-cost average when you invest, minimize your taxes, budget budget budget, and the like. The financial consultants who taught the course did a fine job of conveying the material.

As we attempted to put these customary techniques to work, however, Nancy and I found ourselves quite frustrated. She wanted to write for a living, and her income would thus not be steady, especially in the first few years. I was tiring of brokering commercial real estate and unsure of what lay ahead for me. We both wanted to grow and to grow together, yet the course had instructed us to construct savings programs, insurance programs, investment programs, and a real estate portfolio. How could we direct thousands of dollars into these programs each month when it seemed likely that our income would be quite irregular?

We found ourselves having long, tedious, depressing discussions of how to budget for our life. We found ourselves tense over whether we hit the budget or not. Actually, to be more precise, what we found was that I was tense and I made Nancy tense.

After several months of this, we reached a crossroads: to program or not to program? The price for sticking with custom seemed so high. I knew in my heart that Nancy could write. I'd seen it. Why have her take some job that would impede the development of her talent? As for me, there was no way I was spending the next three or four decades strapped to a job I cared for less and less, just so I could retire from it.

Most importantly, we sensed that we did not have to swear off having enough cash just because we gave up on custom. In fact, as we'll see in Chapter 4, my experience had been that both fulfillment and financial success were direct by-products of departing from custom. My net worth at the time we married was the direct result of having started a sole proprietorship.

When I took this step, many people went out of their way to predict that this departure from custom would cause me to starve. They were wrong by almost seven figures. Imagination, not a budget, had played the key role in my success. My faith in myself was more instrumental than any spreadsheet software.

The financial consultants had said nothing about how ignoring custom could enrich your life. They had said nothing about how embracing custom could cause marital tension. Nancy and I felt as if we were trying to build the Golden Gate Bridge with a spade. We decided we didn't have the right tools for the work at hand, and so we chucked the customs, much to our enduring delight.

Today Nancy writes, I write, we have plenty of funds, and we do not suffer under the influence of a budget-tension-small-life program. That financial planning course taught me a lasting money truth, however: financial custom, and the people you customarily pay for financial advice, often can't help you with either your money or your life.

Following this experience, my sense that my own intuition about money would serve me better than financial custom continued to grow. It had served me well to date, I figured, and it had also served many satisfied clients, so why stop now? Armed with this confidence in my unconventional ideas, I started the California Real Estate Clinic, which became the third key experience in shaping my views on money.

At most real estate brokerages, the agent earns a paycheck only when the deal closes and all the work is completed. By contrast, I set the clinic up so that clients paid me by the hour. I selected this compensation scheme for three reasons. It would give the customers peace of mind, because they would not have to fret about whether my advice was motivated by a desire to close a deal and earn a paycheck. It would save the customers money compared to a commission, because the dirty little secret of the real estate industry is that selling a house doesn't normally take much time. It would also make me a more effective adviser, because I would not have to worry about being paid and because people listen to you more carefully when they are paying you.

This was my hypothesis: Change the money, change the relationship. Or, more articulately, shift how the client and I handle the dollars and we'll improve our relationship, improve both our bankbooks, and feel good about the experience.

The clinic brought me lots of couples as clients. A real estate deal being the full financial exam that it is, I witnessed firsthand how they handled their funds. I noticed that when two partners talked about money, the dynamic of the partner-money-partner triangle sometimes produced startlingly destructive behavior.

One woman, for example, started asking me a question and was cut off in midsentence by her husband. "No-no-no-no-no Janine—listen-to-me!" his voice gunned through the office. He then answered her question incorrectly and raced on to a topic that he considered more important. This couple never purchased a house, but instead divorced.

For the record, the men were not the only ones causing problems. Money is the leading cause of conflict for America's couples, according to a recent Roper Starch Worldwide survey, and my experience was that both sexes were making sizable contributions to the statistic. The problem was that neither sex really understood how money worked.

These couples were sold on buying homes just because they thought it was the thing to do. They had not considered whether this deal would marry them to jobs they would want to leave well before the thirty-year mortgage was paid. They were locked into the savings, retirement, insurance, and investment programs that Nancy and I had been instructed to begin. They were competing with each other to see who earned more income or who exhibited more investment savvy. They often were not listening to me and, in some cases, were not even listening to each other. Most of all, they were moving far too fast. The fallout from their financial habits showed up in both their net worth and their relationships.

Change the money, change the relationship. That was the founding principle of the clinic, so I began going back over my years of experiences and figuring out in great detail which money practices worked and what they yielded. I also became dogmatic about implementing my findings.

Today, for example, no clinic client responds to an offer to purchase a house without practicing money's third fundamental: being deliberate. This means they sleep on the offer at least one night. The buyers don't always like this, their brokers never like it, and sometimes even my clients wonder why I am so rigid on this. The truth, though, is that a deliberate negotiating pace takes much of the stress out of the process. It gives my clients time to consider the offer and to get in sync with each other. It routinely produces benefits they can bank. My clients have saved untold amounts of cash and high blood pressure just from this single practice.

As my research into the fundamentals of money progressed and became part of my work at the clinic, I found more couples taking the time to thank me for my help. "You not only helped us through a tough transaction," the theme seemed to be, "but you taught us some points about money. We never expected this, but it was worth every penny." The most direct signal that this work influenced more than people's bankbooks came at a

Christmas party, when one of my clients told Nancy, "My husband and I were looking for investment advice. We didn't realize we'd get such good marriage counseling, too."

The clinic teaches me a fundamental truth every day: Observe how you handle your dollars, because it impacts your relationship, your bankbook, and your sense of self-worth.

As the clinic became established, I started writing a mystery about a multimillion-dollar pension-fund swindle. A friend pointed out that a novel might be fun to write but that a nonfiction work would probably have more impact on people's lives. Her comment rang true with me. When you read a book about finance, you have to think about the work you do. When you read about careers, you have to be concerned about financing them. When you read about relationships, multiple questions about money and work naturally arise. Based on my experience at the clinic, I could tell that these were not topics that sat tamely in separate compartments as couples traveled together through life. Someone could try to write about life that way, but that was not how it seemed to unfold.

I realized I had more to say than a mystery would carry, so I began making the notes that eventually became *Women, Men, and Money.*

HOW TO USE THIS BOOK

You can use this book in several ways. One is to read it intent on increasing your understanding of how money works. Part I introduces money's four fundamentals: becoming articulate, aware, deliberate, and accomplished. It explains why these principles work, shows in great financial and emotional detail how powerful they are, and supplies practical directions for weaving them into your life. It also identifies specific behavior patterns that you and your partner need to unlearn or avoid, and it explains why those types of behavior will undermine the relationship, wealth, and life you seek.

Part II demonstrates how the fundamentals apply to a variety of common issues, including investments, negotiations, mortgages, retirement, financial crises, and financial control between partners. These chapters show how common approaches to these issues lead you to behavior that costs you cash, disrupts your relationship, generates the financial anxiety you hope to escape, and saddles you with a life that's standard and poor. These chapters illustrate how a disciplined application of the fundamentals leads to decidedly unconventional choices yet strikingly rich rewards. By absorbing this material, you can make yourself a more advanced student of money's fundamentals.

A second option is to use the book as an opportunity to practice employing those fundamentals. Each chapter ends with a set of practices. Many of the practices are specifically geared to help you grasp the material in the chapter. Others are labeled Circuit Training Practices; these will help you work on patterns of behavior that, while not directly related to the chapter, will complement your efforts to use money well.

I invite you to try some of the practices. You can learn a lot from the text without doing them, but they will add a distinct dimension to your understanding of money. They help you break the often intense pressure to accumulate material goods and to conform to financial custom. They also help you work the fundamentals into your life.

Some of the practices may seem completely nonfinancial, and this is intentional. To be more deliberate with money, for example, you must live more deliberately. There's no other way. By slowing down, you increase the likelihood that you will move deliberately under financial pressure. That living more deliberately makes life more pleasant as well as more lucrative is just one of the benefits of mastering the fundamentals.

I recommend you keep a pen with colored ink—not gray, black, or navy blue—as well as a notebook of unlined paper on hand for doing the written work, for noting your experience with the practices that you complete, and for recording your thoughts and questions as you progress through the book. When you finish, go over what you've written and make a list of things to do and topics to discuss with your partner. Don't be surprised at what you discover. You may want to refinance the house, take acting classes, or move to France. You may want to redo some of the practices. By working the practices, you can begin to make the fundamentals your own.

Your third option is to use the book as a reference. I recommend you revisit the fundamentals and the practices from time to time. Once a month is good, and so is anytime you feel flat, anxious, or cornered by a financial difficulty of some sort. Try some of the practices, especially the ones you have skipped over in the past. Reread parts of both the text and your journal. Add to your journal, or start a fresh one if you like.

Returning to the book will remind you of habits you need to embrace. It will refresh you by triggering insights you may not have experienced on earlier trips through the material. Competence with money—or indeed with love and with life—is not a once-and-for-all proposition but rather a matter of uncovering deeper levels of understanding about what you need to do to flourish as human beings, and then doing that. Keep growing.

Working through the book together with your partner is a fine idea, though it is not the only way to profit from the material. You may prefer to work on it separately and compare notes afterward. Solo or ensemble, the point is to employ the fundamentals. Whatever approach you choose, understand that you and your partner may cover and absorb the material at different rates.

In addition, keep in mind that even if you are currently looking forward to a relationship, money's fundamentals still apply. They can help you take care of your bankbook and soul. They can also help you put yourself in a position to find and grow with the love of your life. Don't shelve the book just because you are working on it by yourself for the moment.

How will you know that the fundamentals and the practices are beginning to work? Eventually you will find yourselves feeling less anxious about life's financial details and spending less time grinding away at them. You will find yourselves working your work, or at least taking steps toward that end, and the prospect of a larger income will be on the horizon.

You will feel a deeper appreciation for your partner. You will ask yourself more frequently, "How can I be articulate, aware, deliberate, and accomplished about this issue?" Your life will feel more distinctive and less like it has been cut out of *Money* magazine.

At first, however, the fundamentals may feel awkward and unfamiliar. Keep in mind that they are geared to help you thrive, not to school you in the customs of traditional personal finance.

At times you may be surprised at how much the fundamentals rely on your intuition and your individual talents. Keep in mind that the aim is to choreograph a life that is uniquely and completely your own, not to present you with a recipe for a standardized experience.

At times the fundamentals may also seem to point you away

from money. Understand that they are simply pointing you beyond the dollars and numbers, toward talent, self-esteem, connection, and intimacy and ultimately toward ample material gain. Let go of your preconceptions without relinquishing your desire to thrive.

This book is not about confronting you with that old cliché "Your money or your life" and directing you away from money. That is a formula for a small, unhappy life. Many say that money can't buy love, and while this is true in a literal sense, it does not mean that life and love are important to the exclusion of money. That is a simplistic and weak perspective, one that merely rationalizes incompetence and overlooks money's real power.

This book is also not a guide to cutting deals with extra profit in them. It is not a manual on how to save cash by discovering little-known tax deductions, finding the right mutual funds, or cutting your own hair. Those paths lead to different small, unhappy lives.

You two cannot afford to travel those paths, because you have this work of art—your life together—that you are orchestrating. Money is unavoidably mixed into that life, so instead of trying to ignore it, you need to figure out how to make sure it does not ruin the work. How do you navigate in a way that will support you financially as well as emotionally and spiritually?

To put the question in more explicit terms, assume it is 2:30 P.M. on a sunny Monday in July, and you are experiencing turbulence. Every time your phone rings you think it's the bank calling about the mortgage payment that was due last Thursday. You have just finished a very sharp conversation with your partner about whether this month's preschool tuition check should come out of his account or yours. Earlier today your boss ordered you to leave for Houston and Modesto tomorrow to calm customers angry about the company's troubled software programs. Assume, too, that amid all these demands, you and your partner aspire to a marriage of true minds. What do you do?

This book is what you do.

1 Couples and Money

The Struggle and the Dance

Kathy and Tim used to assume that when they discussed their finances, the task was to debate the merits of their respective viewpoints, then implement the viewpoint that made the most fiscal sense. The problem was, the debates left contusions on their affection, and avoiding the debates held up their life.

"How much to save, how to use the credit cards, how expensive a home to buy—we disagreed on all kinds of stuff," explained Tim. "It was depressing."

In the wake of some counseling, the couple developed a different approach to their finances. Recently Kathy applied to school to earn a teaching credential. She wanted a new blouse just for the interview, an unplanned expense of around $50. Tim's first impulse was to say they couldn't afford it. "Then I remembered that I thought Kathy would be a great teacher and that I wanted her to be accepted into the program," he recalled. Kathy bought the blouse. She was not accepted into that program, but today she teaches for a living.

Hanna and Dennis used to look at a negotiation as a grave battle in which each side fired off lowball offers, hard-line demands, and slick maneuvers in an effort to extract dollars

17

from the other side. They excelled at the nest egg defense: consumed by the thought of future expenses, they tried to wring every penny they could out of every transaction they conducted.

Despite a staunch commitment to their strategy, it rarely produced the results they wanted. They were particularly furious when they had to pay $540 for unexpected termite repairs in order to sell their last home. They thought the buyers should have covered the expense. "We always give in on stuff like that," said Hanna at the time. "I guess that's why we don't have much money."

After a long talk with their attorney, the couple adopted a fresh outlook on their finances. They recently sold a condo they had rented out for several years. The first offer they received was $15,000 under the asking price, and the second was only slightly better. They ignored both offers, partly because the proposals were low, and partly because they were occupied with the arrangements for launching the line of sensible women's shoes that Dennis had been working on for two years. Within a couple of weeks, the two buyers fell into a bidding match, trying to attract the couple's attention, and the condo eventually sold for $1,300 more than the asking price.

What shifted for these couples? They each made a unique commitment. They committed themselves to earning more from money than mere dollars. They started to earn, spend, invest, negotiate, and communicate about money in a way that supported not only their bankbook but also their self-esteem, their relationship, their peace of mind, and their connection with others. They now refuse to do anything strictly for the cash.

Tim and Kathy now discuss finances knowing that having

plenty of cash on hand is more likely when they are also aiming to establish a deep connection with each other and to move through life in sync. Dennis and Hanna now negotiate deals knowing that striking a good one is more likely when they are also aiming to cultivate their talents, their self-worth, and their customers.

These couples stopped letting finances devour them. By committing themselves to earning a richer return from money, they began to use money to flourish as human beings.

Like these couples, you and your partner need to commit yourselves to collecting more than mere dollars from your financial maneuvers. If you do not, you run two risks. The immediate risk is that you will cause yourselves the conflict, the resentment, and the cash flow anxieties you hope to avoid. The long-term risk is that you will never grow together into the rich and meaningful relationship you hope to enjoy.

When you and your partner commit yourselves to reaping money's full rewards, by contrast, you can lift yourselves over the inevitable differences of opinion you two will have about how to handle your funds. When you know how money works, you can earn, spend, invest, and negotiate in a way that will bolster your self-esteem, forge meaningful connections with those you serve with your work, and deposit large sums in your bankbook. When you master money, you can know yourselves better, know each other better, and share your lives in deep and fulfilling ways.

Allowing the money to play such a pivotal role in your life together does not make you a pair of heartless mercenaries. Admitting that handling dollar bills a certain way can yield intangible benefits like intimacy and self-esteem does not make you a pair of dreamy idealists. When you see money without all the myths and customs we have caked on top of it, you simply find that you can use it to generate a lot of cash as you rely on it again and again over the course of your lifetime to connect at the soul.

Many couples think they have made the commitment to obtain a richer return on money when in fact their actions and the results of those actions indicate that they have not. These couples assume that if they can just keep doing their finances the way they always have, they will achieve the rich and satisfying life they seek. In fact, in staying the course, these couples settle for an experience together that is neither rich nor lucrative.

How can you and your partner avoid this painful error? How can you collect all of money's invaluable yield? Contrary to popular belief, couples who use money wisely do not immerse themselves in a state-of-the-art financial plan or concoct 1,001 ways to live on less. Committing yourselves to using money to flourish as a couple begins with understanding two points. First, you need to know why the struggle with money persists. Second, you need to see exactly where the power of money originates.

THE STRUGGLE WITH MONEY

Almost every one of us struggles with money at some point in our lives, regardless of our appetite for personal finance. For some couples money is a matter for constant attention, a full-time job of coupons, budget tinkering, mutual fund comparisons, and income tax tactics. Others take a much looser approach, focusing instead on creating a well-rounded life together. No matter how much attention a couple devotes to money, from time to time something happens—the rent rises, the stock market falls, or one of them bounces a check—and for a moment, and often more, money concerns can consume them.

Interestingly, the amount we have in the bank does not insulate us from the turbulence money can cause. People with no savings fret about losing their jobs and whether they can afford groceries. Billionaires fret about scandals in the bond market and revisions to the Revenue Code. Regardless of your tax bracket, money can produce anxiety. Regardless of your tax bracket, a fight with your partner over how to invest your savings is a fight with your partner. From the most obsessive of us to the most relaxed, from the richest to the poorest, money can rock us all.

Our vulnerability to money problems is hardly surprising. As human beings we need shelter, food, and clothing to survive. For the past five thousand years or so, money has played a key role in our ability to secure these goods. With our survival so clearly at stake and the instrument for ensuring it so frequently puzzling, some struggling is understandable—with money and with each other over money—no matter how deeply we love the ones we're with.

Being sensible people, we all want to cut back on the frustration money causes us and instead use it to build fulfilling lives for ourselves. The question is how to do so in a reliable fashion.

Sometimes couples and their money are clearly in the flow. An attractive job offer materializes. They agree she should take it. They put the house up for sale, and an offer to buy it appears within days. They agree on a negotiating position, and the buyers accept their terms. Escrow closes, they move, and he finds work with good pay within a few weeks. The explanation? "We're in the flow" is all most folks can say. This sounds delicious, but where to find this flow remains a mystery.

More often, it seems, money disrupts a couple's life together. She barks at him for overusing the credit card, he seethes and silently calls her a name, he is weary of comparing mutual funds, she is tired of watching their mutual funds go south, they need a new refrigerator because the old one expired last night, they feel overworked, they feel underpaid, they owe extra taxes because he misread the retirement account instructions. M is for "money," but it can also be for "miserable."

For many of us our erratic track record with money is a very sore spot. You and your partner want to use money in a way that will make your life together surge forward, but often money seems to be equal parts calculus and voodoo, and so exerting any control over it seems impossible. As you think about your track record, you may realize that you keep getting knocked off stride on the same old turns:

THE FRUSTRATING LOOPS IN THE STRUGGLE WITH MONEY

• When you and your partner talk about money, the discussion often leaves one or both of you feeling angry or attacked.

• You sense that financially shrewd people act swiftly, but when you and your partner try to act swiftly, you lose money, get upset, or both.

• You are dissatisfied with your job, yet petrified of losing it.

• You long for more fulfilling work but don't know what it would be, or if you do, you assume that it won't pay enough, that you are incapable of doing it, or that it will not fit into your life together.

• You and your partner compete to see who brings home the biggest paycheck or displays the most investment savvy.

• You invest, but the investments never seem to pay off as richly as you expected.

• When you negotiate on a car, house, job, or loan, you both usually feel as if you lose; when you try to dig in, you feel entirely uncomfortable, you sense that you sound shrill, and the deal often blows apart.

• Just when your finances seem steady, a crisis hits and you two feel pushed to the brink of bankruptcy.

• Your partner views debt as evil; you think differently. This causes friction, but you see no way around it, given your different "money personalities."

• You have run the numbers, and you are both depressed because you are certain you will never have enough money.

• You have—or are en route to having—more money in the bank than you ever thought you would possess, and yet the life you lead seems hollow and unfulfilling.

• You are sick and tired of putting so much time into investing and budgeting without getting ahead, and you feel that something is missing.

Are you and your partner caught in any of these costly and dispiriting loops? If so, you are probably laboring under some common misconceptions about how money works. When you clear these up, you will see that you have much more control over money's impact on your life than you thought. Reaping money's full range of rewards does not have to be a stroke of divine intervention. You can make it happen. To do so, however, you need to understand that the struggle with money persists because the most common techniques for dealing with it rarely succeed.

Solutions That Sell You Two Short

The biggest impediment to harnessing money's power to enhance your life together is that the galaxy is packed with attractive misinformation on how to accomplish the task. This misinformation is available in financial magazines, beauty magazines, Web sites, and fortune cookies. You can receive it from parents, teachers, and others you respect. Large quantities are often obtainable at cocktail parties and in the offices of people you pay to be experts.

No one presses this flawed intelligence on you with the specific intention of disrupting your life. Everyone is doing the best that he or she can. Good intentions aside, however, bad ideas abound.

The common feature of this misinformation is that it gives you the sense that you are handling money well even as it leads you to undermine your relationship, your bankbook, and your peace of mind. If you and your partner are unsure about how money works, you will find it virtually impossible not to be influenced by incomplete or defective wisdom. Three types of programs perpetuate the struggle with money.

THE TRUTHS. Some folks take a principle from a Sunday sermon or a thought that rings true from a counseling session and attempt to guide their finances with that wisdom. This strategy seems sound. You feel comfortable taking a cue from a source with integrity. Your intuition tells you that the wisdom contains elements of truth. But while such wisdom can give you and your partner an admirable objective—embrace prosperity, for example, or talk your money problems through—it rarely includes enough specifics to integrate the principle into your actions with money. Accordingly, on a normal rough-and-tumble financial day, your inspired ideal rarely makes an impact on how you act.

At a break during a workshop I recently led, I asked one of the men attending if any specific issues brought him there that day. He told me that he had asked two women to marry him in recent years, but that both relationships had ended when he informed the women that they would have to sign a prenuptial agreement before the wedding.

In the wake of those events the man had done some work with a therapist on his viewpoint on money. "I'm working on having a different relationship with money," he explained. "I'm focusing more on practicing prosperity and not worrying about my business all the time."

The man went on to explain that he was now planning to propose marriage to his current girlfriend, and he was hoping the workshop would help him figure out the answer to a question that continued to bother him: how could he make the prenuptial seem more palatable this time around?

No matter how fancy a platter you serve it on, a prenuptial agreement always carries a sour taste. This man thought he was developing an enlightened approach to money, but he was about to spoil yet another relationship because he had no idea how to convert his ideals into action. As is often the case with "the truths," he could say the words, but their spirit was getting lost in the translation.

THE MYTHS. Many people allow money myths to dictate their financial actions. Money is evil, all rich people are smart, self-defense is the key to financial success—these are among the numerous beliefs circulating in our culture. These myths are popular because they seem to provide simple explanations for complex experiences. If you are having trouble seeing why you and your partner bicker about money, for example, the belief that money is evil gives you an easy answer, and you can thereafter try to avoid discussing money. If you allow one of these fictions to dictate your behavior, however, the personal pain you invite is sizable.

I recently heard the story of a two-career couple in their thirties who believed in financial self-defense. This school of thought recommends that couples take a let's-get-it-all-on-the-table approach to money. Make finances a common topic of discussion and negotiation, the thinking goes. Investigate how much money your partner has, how much he owes. Check her credit rating to make sure she has no bad debts. Credit reports. Disclosure. In theory these measures will safeguard your individual assets and promote an open, honest relationship.

Swayed by this school of thought, the young couple decided that fairness demanded they split their finances. They tracked everything from the down payment on their home to expenses for groceries, haircuts, and houseplants. They knew at all times who owned what percentage of which investment. In time, these records became a way to compete to see who was contributing the most to the marriage. When their relationship began to deteriorate, they each worked harder to earn more, because the records had become the only way they judged their contributions to the marriage.

How well did the idea of financial self-defense serve this couple? They had a smaller net worth when they divorced than when they married, so it hardly made them rich. And while the myth did not cause their divorce, it introduced an adversarial posture to their relationship from the outset. The myth put distance between them, then kept it there.

The couple believed that financial self-defense would strengthen their life together. What they discovered is that marriage is not a martial art. Like most money myths, financial self-defense can be dangerous nonsense.

THE MATH. A third option you and your partner have for solving money problems is to let the numbers be your exclusive guide. The logic here seems beyond dispute: you know you will have expenses, so if you can eliminate some of your bills and make sure you have sufficient funds to pay the rest, most of your money problems will be solved. For many folks this logic takes shape in a most traditional approach to money: get a job, buy a house, and save for retirement.

Jack and Helen followed this formula. He was an architect; she was a paralegal. They raised two children in a house they now own free and clear. They excelled at economizing, tracking their investments, and minimizing their income taxes.

Theirs has not been a bad life and certainly has not been without good times and substance as well as an ample retirement account. But Helen thinks she could have been a great marriage and family counselor. Jack wishes he could have been a college professor and watercolor artist. As Helen thinks back over the life they've led, she sees it as busy, safe, comfortable, and small, and the more she thinks about it, the angrier she feels.

How much better would she feel about herself had she pursued her talents as a counselor? What lessons would this have conveyed to their children about developing their own talents? How much more money would they have? What more would have been possible for Helen and Jack's relationship had they each pursued their vision? Grants, university appointments, books, showings, perhaps being faculty members together, trips, conferences—none of these possibilities ever became a reality because the two of them never believed in themselves enough to take life's most interesting risks. Despite almost four decades of marriage, on some level Jack and Helen have yet to know each other, because their finances have kept them from growing into the people they sense they could be.

A lifetime by the numbers—regular paychecks, regular investment, regular mortgage payments—can produce success for you by many of the standards held out today. Helen and Jack, however, would contend that those standards are set too low and that clearing them will not satisfy you. They would tell you that a fulfilling life together is a creation, not an algebra problem. They would say that when you live by the numbers, your life together usually adds up, but it does not add up to what it could.

Checking for Signs of Struggle

Think back to the frustrating financial loops listed at the outset of this section. Are you and your partner caught up in any of them? If so, chances are good that you are suffering from a case of the truths, the myths, or the math.

Do a little checking here, and be honest with yourself. By Monday lunch, have the truths you listened to over the weekend at temple or in church been overwhelmed by your business or job? Examine your assumptions about money. Do you look at it as a game? A necessary evil? A skill that some are born with and some are not? Pause for a moment and consider whether your finances leave you feeling as if you are running on a hamster wheel.

Don't lose heart if these symptoms sound all too familiar. With all the incomplete and defective financial advice that swirls around us, it's easy to fall for a program that lulls you into thinking that you are taking care of your money concerns as well as possible. Understand, however, that the truths, the myths, and the math merely perpetuate the struggle with money. There's no way to do them better and achieve improved results. These programs don't help you commit to using money well. They keep your life and your relationship from growing the way you hope they will. They also cost you cash.

How do you and your partner break out of these destructive habits and move into a nourishing flow with money? To stop selling yourselves short and start living larger, you need to understand that the real power behind money does not lie in the possession of dollar bills. The real power originates in an entirely different spot.

THE COMMITMENT THAT DISSOLVES THE STRUGGLE

Simone and Jean Claude recently renovated the spare bedroom in their house so that Jean Claude would have a studio in which to write children's books. They hired Sam to design and construct the renovation. Sam suggested that a skylight would make the room more inviting, and though this would add $1,000 to the cost, the couple thought it was a good idea.

When the contract for the work arrived, Simone noticed that it was for only $900 more than the estimate on the design sans skylight. Sam told her, "My daughter has one of your husband's books and really likes it, so at ten bucks apiece, I'm buying her and her friends the first ten copies of the next one."

On the day Sam arrived to reframe the roof and the back wall, Jean Claude nudged Simone and called to the contractor, "Hey, nice jacket."

"Thanks," replied Sam. "My wife gave me this five years

ago, and it keeps me warmer and drier than anything I've ever had." Simone explained to Sam that his cobalt-blue biking jacket was one of her firm's first big sellers. She then made a note to herself to consider bringing back that style in updated colors.

Simone earns a six-figure annual income from the sportswear firm she owns, but it was not always thus. In the firm's second year, the bills were piling up, the couple's savings balance was dropping, and the business seemed stalled. At that time Jean Claude's income from his writing was quite uneven, so the couple's financial picture seemed bleak.

They talked several times that year about whether Simone should fold the firm and just find a designing job at one of the large sportswear companies. The idea seemed logical, yet they concluded each discussion feeling that she should continue designing and selling her own work.

"I had this gut feeling that I could produce better and more valuable pieces working on my own," said Simone, "and Jean Claude kept saying we should follow my instincts."

"There were months when I had no idea how we'd pay the bills," recalled Jean Claude, "but Simone is so talented that I knew something good would come of her work."

Lean times continued through year two. Simone continued to work. Midway through year three came a turning point: a national retailer bought a line of running shorts and tops. Since then, sales have increased, not always smoothly but at least to the point where the firm is now a clear success.

Look at the richness of the life this couple has created. They both earn a living practicing the craft that they chose and for which they have talent. Developing this expertise adds muscle to their self-esteem and provides the material support for their life together.

Both of them can connect to other people through the exchanges they make with clients like Sam, earning the sense that they have helped someone else in an important and valuable way. They also receive the same kind of meaningful help in return. In this way they enhance the comfort of knowing that they are not alone in the world.

Finally, thanks to their approach to money, Jean Claude and Simone enhance their relationship. Jean Claude is fascinated by his wife's designing. He is proud of her and inspired by her, and he feels lucky that he shares his life with such a gifted person.

Simone is equally proud of Jean Claude's writing, and she's grateful for the time he took off to help her start her firm. She feels good that they appreciate each other's talent and support each other. They are both happy about the atmosphere this creates for their children and the lessons it teaches them about how to build a life.

This is a distinctive standard of living. Had their financial discussions focused solely on the level of their net worth, they probably would have opted for a safer, smaller course, and they would not have forged the strong bond they share today. Had they earned a comparable amount of money through stock speculation or jobs that meant less to them, the return from their finances would have been much less. The work that generated the income would not have come from deep within them, and their connection to clients would not be so deep, their self-esteem would not be as well developed, and they would not be sharing a life that means as much to them. Their financial efforts would have yielded income and little else. Even if those efforts had yielded an enormous income, they could not have purchased intimacy, self-worth, and connection to others, because those must be earned day by day, not bought.

What exactly did they do to earn this life? Are they just risk-takers who were lucky enough to have their gambles pay off? In fact, they are much more accomplished than that. Note two points about their life.

First, note what they did. They worked on themselves—on her designing and his writing, on loving each other and themselves, and on finding ways to take care of customers. The cash, the intimacy, the self-worth, and the security they enjoy—these are a result of having given expression to the talent, spirit, and vision within them, of having liberated their human promise. Their experience illustrates an important point: a commitment to tapping money's richness is a commitment to fulfilling our promise as human beings. It is not a matter of dominating others or controlling large blocks of funds. Couples thrive because they live the life they are capable of, individually and together.

Simone and Jean Claude understand that we don't acquire money's multifaceted yield just because we've got a dollar—or even a truckload of them—in our pockets. They understand that money is an instrument of personal evolution and that the power of it lies not in taking permanent possession of the funds but in how we behave with them. The fortune is coined of us, not by us. When we earn, spend, invest, negotiate, and communicate with a commitment to fulfilling our promise, we convert the talent, spirit, and vision within us into the rich life we desire. All the power, all the richness, comes from within.

Living the Vow at Every Moment

Second, note that this couple's commitment to a higher standard of living was not a onetime event. To create their life they had to reaffirm their commitment to fulfilling their promise many times over. This means that they had to learn how to let go and hang on.

When Simone realized that she could design clothes that people found valuable, she had to let go of her former goals and commit to bringing forth this new vision of herself. When Jean Claude realized that she needed his help, he had to let go of the notion that he would write every week for the rest of his life, yet hang on to his promise as a writer and have faith that he would return to writing.

As life unfolded, the couple had to be willing to let go of many things: the assumption that income should arrive in identical amounts twice a month; the expectation that savings should rise in a perfectly uninterrupted upward slope; the idea that they could not earn large sums of money; and their expectations about how fast their progress should be and how much work it should take, to name just a few. Through the ebb and flow of all these circumstances, though, the two of them hung on to their promise. By dancing with their promise in this way, by reaffirming their commitment to it at every juncture, they have achieved success in one of its broadest and most satisfying forms.

Jean Claude and Simone do not have an unusual tolerance for risk. They have an unswerving commitment to their own growth, to becoming the people they are capable of becoming. Thanks to the way they use money, they have been able to grow together.

INFINITE RICHES IN AN INTIMATE DANCE

How can you and your partner craft a life as rich as Simone and Jean Claude's? To succeed with money, you need to devote yourself to fulfilling your human promise as if your life depends on it, because it does. At every financial turn, be squarely and immediately engaged in your own evolution.

The stakes here are high: not pursuing your promise is the root of the struggle with money. Unless you are wedded to the idea of making good on your promise, you will never make the money moves that will allow you to flourish. You will instead find yourself trapped in the loops you hope to avoid.

When you are not committed to creating a deep bond between the two of you, for example, it's easy to lurch into jousting with each other over a $50 blouse and to feel angry and attacked during your discussions.

When you are not focused on developing your talents, it's easy to labor far longer than is healthy in a job that doesn't suit you, to feel dissatisfied with that job yet petrified of losing it, and to feel underpaid.

When you are not devoted to doing valuable work for people, it's easy to fall into protracted haggling with a home buyer over a $540 termite repair and to feel as if you lose every negotiation you enter.

In such instances you fail to honor the most essential elements of yourself, and the price you pay is steep. Your talent sits untapped, and your self-esteem languishes. You miss out on the cash that your talents could have generated, and your connection with the people you serve weakens. Your relationship suffers, and time slides away from you. Nothing will compensate you for any of these losses.

When you don't commit yourselves to using money to fulfill your promise, it's easy to slip into doing life strictly for the dollars. This is desperate and self-defeating. It is the root of financial insecurity and economic anxiety: you essentially lose track of your most valuable assets—the two of you.

When you acknowledge your promise and make a commitment to fulfilling it, by contrast, you and your partner put yourselves in a position to flourish. The fact is that you, like Simone and Jean Claude, are too talented and too magnificent to be consumed for even a split second by $50, $540, or any other sum. The richness is all inside you, and your task in life is to do the work of bringing it forth.

You will have to let go to hang on to that promise. A boss, a teacher, or a family member may at one time have told you that you had little talent. You'll have to stop assuming he was right.

It may be your habit to make all the important financial decisions in your relationship. This habit will have to go.

Your income may dip as you true up your course. You two will need to release yourselves from the fear that it will never go up again.

You may hit setbacks and dry spells. You will have to let go of your frustration and use your imagination to conceive of a different path. Several times.

You or your partner may find that you simply have no sense of what your promise is. You will have to let go of the assumption that this means you don't have any promise so that you can begin to catch a glimpse of it.

Keep in mind that fulfilling your promise is not a sprint or a prizefight. It is more of a dance—between the two of you and within each one of you.

As you become more competent at bringing forth this richness, you'll build a sense of security that will withstand even the most fickle turn of financial events. You'll find yourselves able to negotiate impressive deals and substantial incomes. You will realize that you have valuable contributions to make to other people's lives, and you'll create a life of distinction and service. You will feel the inspiration that comes from watching your partner grow, as well as the inspiration that comes from having her support you.

Eventually you will see the simple, powerful truth: the more you surrender to the talent, vision, and spirit within you, the more you'll evolve and achieve greatness as human beings. This greatness is who you are, this greatness is what enables you to form an exquisite relationship with your partner, and this greatness, along with a fine bankbook, is what money is designed to help you cultivate.

A Renaissance for Two

To achieve the relationship to which you and your partner aspire, you must use money well. The key is not to exclude money from your life, to discover the right program for managing money, or to contrive a way to insulate your relationship from the stress you let money cause you. The key is to be yourselves more fully than ever before.

The question, of course, is how to earn, spend, invest, negotiate, and communicate about money on a daily basis so that this personal renaissance can materialize. In the din generated by all the talk of retirement plans, downsizings, hidden mutual fund fees, and how much life insurance will really be enough, you two can easily lose track of exactly how to use money most powerfully. Money can become very complex when your broker is urging you toward more investment risk, the boss is telling you to work harder, and you can hear your grandmother's voice in the back of your head repeating that money is evil.

How do you handle money in a way that will keep your commitment to secure money's full range of rewards? Day in and day out, how do you use your funds to keep your commitment to fulfill your promise?

You practice the fundamentals of money.

PRACTICE

1. Name your two best uses of money ever. Any instance in which you earned, invested, spent, or negotiated for money is a candidate. Why were these experiences so remarkable? Were these cases in which the lasting benefits extended beyond mere cash? If not, name a time when you earned more than dollars from your money.

2. Name your two worst uses of money ever. Again, any instance in which you earned, invested, spent, or negotiated for money is a possibility. What made these experiences so unsatisfying? Were these instances in which you were aiming strictly for dollars? Name a time when you acted strictly for the money, and figure out how you could have acted differently and improved your yield.

3. List twenty reasons why you have value as a person. List your assets and their location.

Circuit Training

1. Describe in three sentences or less how you earn money now. If you are not earning money regularly at this moment, describe how you earned it most recently or how you expect to earn it at your next opportunity.

2. List five really great things you think you could do for people—services you could provide or products you could supply—if you had the resources and opportunity.

3. Take your partner on a date. Make it fun and inexpensive. A trip to the zoo or the beach is good, and so is anything else simple that you love to do. Live music is excellent. Bring along a picnic basket or stop off for a favorite food. Revel in the luxury of this. Turn this event into a weekly affair.

4. Spend thirty minutes sprucing up your desk at work. Spend another thirty minutes on some part of your home. Take a spirited approach: rearrange, refresh, clean up, and toss.

5. Buy some cut flowers for your home this week.

6. What do you do for exercise? Perhaps you walk, swim, or cycle, or maybe you are considering yoga, weight lifting, or working out at a gym. Be disciplined about making time for gaining the self-esteem that comes from working out. If you have no regimen or want to step up your intensity, consult your physician about how to proceed.

The Four
Fundamentals
of Money

I

2 The Value of Being Articulate

Denise and Mike entered their lawyer's office talking about how relieved they were that someone had finally made an offer to buy their house. Denise then handed their attorney the offer and said, "Here's our biggest question: can we get the buyer to increase his deposit by, say, three or four—"

"No, Denise. That's not our biggest question," Mike broke in testily. "Our biggest question is whether we can get the buyer to make a higher offer."

Denise didn't budge. "No, Michael. That's not the biggest question, because we know we're not going to get more money."

"We don't know that," Mike shot back, leaning into his wife's face for emphasis. "He might pay another ten thousand dollars if we are smart enough to ask for it."

Despite repeated advice to reconvene at a calmer time, Mike and Denise insisted on making a counteroffer that morning. Distorted by their desire to prove each other wrong, their proposal contained a number of unrealistic terms, and the buyer, predictably, rejected it.

What did the couple have to show for their financial efforts? They lost a good opportunity to sell their house and move on with their lives, and they wasted the fee they paid for legal advice. They also created at least one full morning of mutual animosity for themselves.

Many couples like Denise and Mike work very hard at earning, saving, and investing their funds, hoping to improve their lives. Unfortunately their financial focus often overlooks an important truth: when partners don't know how to talk about money, they pay for it in their relationship and at the bank.

The big mistake these couples make is that both partners insist on being right when they discuss finances. These couples miss the point. Committing to a broader return on money requires a broader perspective. The object of talking about money is to figure out what action will help you create a fulfilling life together. The most significant part of the endeavor is to connect with your partner, not to have your way.

Being articulate is the first fundamental of money because it is so essential to helping you make this connection. If Mike and Denise had understood how to be articulate about money, they could have created a very different experience for themselves. They could have acknowledged their differing viewpoints of the offer and then also acknowledged their shared desire to sell their home and move into a larger one to accommodate their growing family. They could have stepped toward completing their move and refocusing their energy on developing their talents, raising their children, and nourishing their relationship. They could also have avoided wasting several hundred dollars in attorney fees.

Unfortunately, like many couples, Denise and Mike see any money discussion as a contest in which the object is to ensure that one opinion prevails over another. I think the offer is bad, their thinking goes, and thus I don't want to accept the offer, and I will say what I must to my partner to have my way.

If you take this type of adversarial stance in money discussions with your mate, you will risk having your relationship fall into one of three destructive and costly patterns.

COMBAT. In some cases both partners cling stubbornly to their positions. These folks spar freely over money and inflict emotional and financial wounds on themselves, much as Denise and Mike did when they discussed the purchase offer.

RETREAT. One partner may tire of clashing over finances, or she may avoid them altogether from the start. She may abandon her position whenever her partner opposes it. Marlene, for example, gives in to Pete on virtually every money decision they make. Pete's job prospects have determined where they have lived and when they have moved for ten years, even when moving meant that Marlene had to give up a good job to follow him. Pete's risk tolerance dictates which mutual funds they choose and how much they invest in them. Pete has the last word on what kind of car Marlene drives, which home improvements they make, and how much they spend on vacation. Marlene used to fight some of these battles, but now she says, "I ask once, but if he's going to obsess about it, it's just not worth it to me to pursue the argument."

What could she have earned had her work and the development of her talent been accorded more respect in their relationship? She doesn't know. What would their life be like if she had more of a voice in their finances? She doesn't know. How long before Marlene acts on her pent-up resentment, and what will she do then? She doesn't know.

EXILE. Finally, sometimes out of ignorance and sometimes out of battle fatigue, many partners keep their finances entirely separate and almost never discuss them. Pat thinks Ben is a spendthrift, and she's still bitter over the $4,000 credit card bill he ran up back when they were combining their finances. Ben remembers all the carping and criticism that Pat has aimed at his money skills over the years. After twelve years of clashing over money, Pat and Ben steer clear of financial conversations and divide all their expenses between their separate financial worlds.

This silent separation of finances has produced an odd gridlock in their lives: neither one has been able to take the risk of switching to more satisfying and potentially more lucrative work because their arrangement calls for each one to come up with half of the mortgage payment every month. Even taking vacations has become a problem for them, because they rarely have enough extra cash at the same time.

What can you do to keep yourself and your partner from slipping into one of these damaging patterns? How can you make money decisions that will nourish your relationship, build your bankbook, and bring you peace of mind? Conversational etiquette alone will not be enough. You must learn to be articulate.

The key to talking calmly and fruitfully about money is to remind yourselves that negotiation is the process of creating and navigating a future; it is not just an opportunity to horse-trade for a larger spending allowance. Understanding this point fully will keep you from collapsing the discussion into a mad dash to be right.

You will find that the two of you can maintain this enlightened perspective if you divide your money discussions into three distinct phases.

SET UP A CONNECTION

One day recently one of my clients and I decided to cease working together, something that had not happened with me in the past. That same day a new client called to set up some work with my real estate clinic, and a partner at a local firm called to ask if I would conduct a negotiating workshop for his employees.

I went home that evening not sure whether I should feel troubled or elated about my day. A few minutes after I arrived, my wife, Nancy, and I started to prepare dinner for ourselves and our daughter, Amanda. As Nancy chopped vegetables and I set Amanda in her high chair, I tried talking about my day. About three minutes into my story the phone rang, and Nancy handled a quick call from a neighbor. I then continued my tale as I tried to maneuver around Nancy and her chopping block to get a can of SpaghettiOs for Amanda.

As I told Nancy of my mixed emotions about the departed client, I poured some of the pasta into Amanda's dish and extended it toward her. As it got to her, I turned to Nancy to emphasize a point and never noticed Amanda's hand go up. I did hear her say, "No skettios," though, as the bowl came out of my hand and bounced on the floor. That's when I finally realized that telling my story would have to wait.

A poorly timed money discussion is almost guaranteed to be an unsatisfying money discussion. Here are three steps for optimizing your timing.

Pick Your Spot

You can handle simple reminders and requests on the fly—for example, "I have a tough day ahead, so would you mind paying these bills?" or "Did you put money into the checking account?" Just remember to be thoughtful and polite.

For larger topics, however—whether to buy a house, how much to put into savings, unexpected expenses, or a desire to change what you do for work—you want to choose your spot more carefully.

Obviously this choice alone will not guarantee a fruitful discussion, but some choices give you a particularly poor chance of success. Take note.

POOR TIMES AND PLACES
TO DISCUSS MONEY

1. When you have just come home and your partner is feeding the baby and cooking dinner
2. While changing the oil in the car
3. While the children are tugging on you to play soccer
4. After 10:00 P.M.
5. At a bar in front of friends
6. On the phone between appointments at work
7. In the middle of a Saturday afternoon bike trip
8. On date night
9. As one of you is ready to run out the door to a tennis game or to go to work
10. With the television or the radio on

Nancy and I often discuss important money issues when we are parked comfortably on the couch after dinner and after

Amanda has gone to sleep. Another good spot for us is in the car on a longish drive of thirty minutes or more, as long as it doesn't involve a lot of stop-and-go traffic.

You and your partner may feel that the couch and the car are not the right places for your money discussions. You may prefer a half-hour walk. Talk it over and come up with your own ideas. Look for spots where time, attention, and comfort intersect. If you put yourselves in a good position to connect, your discussions will be more fruitful.

Pick Your Topic

Several years ago I received a call from a man who wanted an appointment to meet with me. When I asked what he wished to discuss, he said he wanted me to show him all the homes on the San Francisco Peninsula that were available for under $400,000, negotiate a new lease on his office space, and teach him enough about the California Real Estate Clinic so that he could work for me.

I put more than a little effort into dissuading him from making an appointment because I really didn't want to talk to someone with a sport utility vehicle full of topics on his mind.

What's true for me is probably true for your partner, too: she can handle only so much in one conversation. When deciding on a topic, think small. Don't terrify the audience with the scope of your topic.

Perhaps you are concerned about overspending, whether to pay an accountant to do your taxes this year, hefty charge card balances, and whether to sell the Chevron stock because their Russian oil deal looks weak. These are all valid topics, but announcing that you want to cover them all at one sitting will probably drive your partner out to mow the lawn.

What about your budget for the next twenty years? Will your child's college fund be ripe fifteen years from now? After a very short period of time people's eyes tend to glaze over when such massive topics are brought up.

Here's another scary opener: "I'm tired of how you keep working so much, then spend money at the club. If you really loved me, you wouldn't do that." As a subject, this mixes entirely different issues—whether you are in love, whether your expenditures are wise ones, and whether one of you works too much.

Have a specific topic in mind for discussion:

"Our monthly expenses seem too high to me."
"What adjustments can we make to afford Bobby's braces?"
"I feel trapped when you leave only a few dollars in the checking account each week."
"What are we going to do about health insurance?"

Each one of these is enough for a single discussion. Pick a topic and stick to it.

Ask for the Floor

The other basic step for setting up an articulate discussion about money is to ask your partner if he is willing to have the conversation. Even if you have picked a poor spot, this can make up for it. Your partner may be in the right frame of mind, setting notwithstanding, or she may see that this is a poor time and suggest an alternative. If you have picked a bad topic, she may narrow it down and put you on stride. In this respect all your preparations give you multiple chances either to set a good stage for conversation or keep you from starting one that has little chance of ending well.

Start off with a basic question:

"I would like to talk about our expenses for a moment. Is now a
   good time?"
"You know, we have to decide whether to buy another CD at the
   end of the month or just leave our money in savings. Can we sit
   down for a minute so I can tell you what I've been thinking?"

If your partner tells you, "No, now is not a good time," respect
this and ask for another time. Forcing him to talk when he has
something else on his mind will not yield good conversation.

Once your partner tells you he is ready to talk, remember
that you have the floor. If he interrupts, don't respond by interrupting him. Wait until he finishes, then remind him that you
have the floor:

"I think we can take care of this more smoothly if I finish what I
   have to say and then listen to your thoughts. Is that okay?"
"You might want to hear the rest of what I have to say before you
   make up your mind."

If he asks questions when you pause between thoughts, answer
them if they fit into the flow of your thinking. If they disrupt
your thinking or if he starts to respond to your comments at
these junctures, simply tell him you'd like to finish your
thoughts and then you'll answer all his questions and listen to
everything he has to say. Full expression is what will make you
feel best and keep the discussion fruitful.

Express Yourselves

Once you have set up a discussion, the next task is for each of
you to communicate clearly, completely, and without attacking
each other.

Note that you don't have to make any decisions in this phase. That comes later. We saw in the previous section that a large part of setting up a discussion consists of making sure not to start it prematurely. Similarly, a large part of expressing yourself consists of making sure not to start navigating too soon.

You can also set aside your worries about being right or prevailing in the face of your partner's opposing viewpoint. The work for now is for each of you to say what you feel and tell what you know. This will feel good all by itself, and it will give you the best chance to resolve your differences—or to recognize that you have no differences—and to move smoothly on with life.

To be as articulate as possible and to be heard, follow these guidelines.

Practice the Grammar of Money

Your partner is a good person. He must be; otherwise you would not share your life with him.

Since your partner is a good person, any statement that makes him feel he is a bad person causes trouble for you in two ways: it communicates a thought you do not intend, and it triggers a defensive posture and retaliatory comments from him. The armor and all the superfluous communication then get in your way as you try to discuss your real interest—the money and what the two of you should do about it.

Even when we are quite upset, it is easy to remember not to make obviously incendiary remarks like "You are being an imbecile about how we handle the checkbook," or "You have the investment sense of an empty Coke can." Unfortunately many statements that seem much safer than these can insult your partner just as thoroughly.

Suppose, for example, that Rick objects to Kendra's behavior and decides to tell her, "That mutual fund you picked sure stinks." At first blush this statement seems to carry an honest, simple, and direct message while aiming criticism at the fund, not at Kendra. If you look more closely, however, you will see that the statement does none of these.

What is Rick really trying to say here? Is he nervous about the fund's performance, or does he feel manipulated because Kendra picked the fund without consulting him or without according his opinion enough weight? His word choice makes it impossible to tell.

Instead of being simple and direct, Rick's statement is confusing. Instead of being honest, it is lazy. In its flip and imprecise form, it is a wad of negative input aimed at Kendra. Not being able to tell what Rick's real intention is, her natural impulse will be to retaliate for this salvo, and instead of initiating a thoughtful discussion, Rick's statement will have laid the groundwork for an argument.

To eliminate this sort of needless and harmful distraction, love the person and object to his action with your sentence structure. Break your sentences into feelings and behavior: "I love you very much, and I love our life together. I feel manipulated, though, by the way you took our money out of our savings account without asking me and invested it in the mutual fund."

The key to formulating this type of sentence is to start sentences with "I feel [adjective]" and end them by describing behavior. If you skip the adjective, you are likely to say something such as "I feel that you manipulate me." This kicks off the charge and countercharge loop you hope to avoid: you are saying he intentionally manipulates you on an ongoing basis, a charge that will spark a very different exchange than a statement that a particular action made you feel manipulated at a certain moment.

In addition to keeping you from lobbing inflammatory statements at your partner, this form of statement will force you to clarify what you think. Are you nervous about the family investments, or do you feel manipulated by your wife, or both? If you feel manipulated, exactly what action has made you feel that way?

When you know exactly what troubles you, you can tell your partner about it without raising issues that don't trouble you. This increases the likelihood that you can deal with the real issue swiftly and completely and then move on.

••

The Grammar of Money

••

Reflex Statement	**Articulate Alternative**
You are manipulative.	I felt manipulated when you left only eight dollars in the checking account.
I feel upset when you are unappreciative.	I felt unappreciated when you made fun of my salary in front of Jack and Sue.
The way you keep our charge cards from me makes me feel you are an inconsiderate person.	I feel incompetent when you don't allow me to handle the charge cards.

I feel the problem is that you love your job, not me.	I feel neglected when you spend Saturdays at work instead of with me.
You have no idea what I do to earn the money that runs this house.	I feel unappreciated when you say that all I do is sit at my desk all day.
This broker of yours is an idiot.	I feel very uncomfortable with Don's advice.
You have mismanaged our money.	I am very anxious about the investments you have selected for us.

••

Share Your Opinion About the Money

Jackie and Don recently decided to have their house and garage painted. Don hired the painters without a written contract. He also paid their invoice when it arrived, which was before they started painting the garage. Jackie thought both these moves were mistakes, but she remained silent. A week after the house was finished, Don called to ask when the men would return to do the garage. The owner responded that the price didn't include the garage. "I am furious that this has happened, but it's my own fault," Jackie lamented. "I should have spoken up."

There are two important reasons to tell your partner your opinions about your finances. The first is that if you don't share these opinions, you may regret it later. In his zeal to own a duplex, for example, your partner might not realize that if it sits vacant for several months, covering its mortgage could eat up all your savings. Or perhaps you see how a small loan could support the family while you start your own firm, an option your partner would never consider because his father told him that debt is evil.

You may not feel qualified to offer opinions on some financial issues, but if they will affect your life, I assure you that you are. To get where you are in life, you have surely earned and spent some money. If you have ever put money into a savings account or an educational course, you have invested. If you've ever accepted a job, you have negotiated. You also have intuition, common sense, and the right to change your mind later. With all of this experience and horsepower behind you, you are perfectly qualified to express an opinion about your finances.

Note, too, that you are entitled to have that opinion be completely and uniquely yours. Don't tell your partner what you think you are supposed to say in order to appear financially astute. There is no financial gospel, no matter what you read in the *Wall Street Journal, Money,* or the brochures from your brokerage company.

Don't tell your partner what she wants to hear, either. Just because she knows more about disability insurance or earns more money than you does not mean that your financial opinions carry less weight than hers. A healthy relationship is a partnership of equals. Understand that the two of you may disagree on financial issues, and don't be threatened by that. You can handle any disagreements when it comes time to navigate.

This is your life that you are creating with your money. The two opinions that count most are yours and your partner's, so make sure you do your half of the work.

RICK: I feel nervous about our mutual fund investment. I
         don't want to lose our money, and I have no idea

whether the risks the managers of that fund take
are really appropriate for us.

KENDRA: But I chose this fund because it has been the
highest-performing fund in the country for the past
three years.

RICK: I understand that you think the fund is well
managed and likely to grow. You are not a bad
person for choosing it. I'm just saying that I am
not persuaded that this is a good place for our
money at this point in our lives.

The other reason for sharing your opinion on financial issues is
that it will help you avoid statements that will confuse your
partner and possibly annoy or hurt her.

Suppose, for example, that Rick tosses out a question:
"Don't you know what a mutual fund is?" All this question
does is play keep-away with his opinion. What is *his* understanding of mutual funds? What does *he* think of them? Why is
this information important to the conversation? Rick's word
choice brings these questions up without answering them. He
thus brings confusion to the conversation instead of communication.

Furthermore, this cross-examining style suggests that he
knows the answers to these questions but is quizzing Kendra
about her knowledge. No one likes to be tested for intelligence
in the middle of a conversation, and Rick will be lucky if
Kendra does not resent his remark.

A more articulate expression would look like this: "Mutual
funds buy shares of public companies. I have no idea what the
risks are of owning the shares of these companies, and I do not
have the time to research the issue, so I don't think this is a
good place for us to put our money."

Sharing your opinion about the money also helps you avoid making lazy assertions. If you tell your partner, "Fidelity's funds are for the birds," and offer no more than this, you have not shared your opinion. Without further explanation this clipped construction simply gives the impression that anyone who disagrees with you is unbalanced. If your partner does not share your view, this implication can only cause turbulence that your discussion can do without.

••

Share Your Opinion About the Money

••

Reflex Statement	**Articulate Alternative**
I don't know.	Based on what I've seen, 30 percent off a new baby grand piano strikes me as a real bargain.
It's up to you.	That seems to me like a lot of money to pay for life insurance.
The real estate agent says take it.	I wonder if we could do better if we wait for another offer.
I suppose I should just be happy I have a job.	For the amount of work I do, $32,000 is not a large salary.
I know the economy does not seem too good right now.	I think I can earn more money baking pies than I do working in the sneaker factory.
No one wants an adjustable loan in this market.	My fear with an adjustable loan is that interest rates will go up significantly because of the gov-

	ernment's budget and deficit problems, causing our loan payment to soar.
Selling a house now is a stupid idea.	With the demand for homes so low, it seems to me that we will get a very low price for the house if we try to sell it now.

....

Ask Without Pushing

The third guideline for expressing yourself articulately is to ask for what you want. The straightforward part of your task here is to ask for agreement on a specific action:

"I would like to see us move the money from the mutual fund into the savings account. Can we do that?"

"I would like to see us leave at least $250 in the checking account at all times. What do you think of that?"

Asking for a specific action accomplishes two aims. First, it gives you the best chance of getting what you want without having to repeat a conversation. If Rick does not specifically ask to close the mutual fund account, Kendra, for example, may say, "Okay, I won't put any more money in the mutual fund account." This response doesn't take care of the anxiety that prompted Rick to discuss the issue in the first place, but it forces Kendra to give in twice: once to concede this point and once to do what Rick really wants—take the funds out of the mutual fund account.

Similarly, if you only say, "I'd like to see us be better with the checkbook," your partner may simply say, "Okay." This may be an honest remark and it may be followed by honest effort, but it is no assurance of anything, which means you may well have to have this discussion again next week.

Adding a specific request to your conversation also accomplishes a second aim: it keeps you from sounding as if you are complaining without having put any effort into figuring out a solution. Consider the lack of a request in these statements:

"I need $300 for a suit."
"With all the work you are doing, you don't seem to spend time with me anymore."

Bald statements such as these simply drop a problem in your partner's lap and indicate that you expect him to fix it. Whether you want him to fix the problem or not, a more gracious request is appropriate.

The subtler key to asking for what you want is to make sure you don't push for it. Note how each of these statements pushes, either by demanding certain actions or dictating your partner's behavior:

"I'm going to close out the fund account tomorrow and put the money back in the bank."
"If you don't do it, I'll open a separate account for my paychecks."
"I'm putting $250 in the checking account tomorrow."
"Honey, I've decided our vacation budget this year should be $1,500."
"I'm going to buy a new blouse today."

Whether you push for what you want on purpose or by mistake, you interfere with communication in three ways. First, you alienate your partner just because you pushed. He may not disagree with you, but he may balk at your proposal anyway. Note that while at some point you may have to take independent action—take money out of an account or tell the painters to stop until you have a written contract, for instance—you don't have to talk about that now. For now you can do without any threats.

Second, remember you want the solution to stick. If you want her to stop playing the mutual fund market behind your back, it would be best if she complied because she sees that this behavior hurts your relationship and because she wants the relationship to be good. If you push her into acquiescing, you can never be sure the problem will not reappear or surface somewhere else in your financial world.

Finally, loosening your grip on the outcome of your requests opens up interesting possibilities. If your expression helps him understand your position in a way he never could before, he may take care of your concern better than you could have imagined by offering to do something totally different from what you asked.

"Well, you know, I've been thinking that this is a pain, too. Why don't we put $1,000 in there, not just $250, and have that as our cushion?"

"I've been thinking that this is a pain, too. Why don't we close out the entire brokerage account and focus on building up our work?"

Don't limit yourself by clinging too tightly to a single outcome.

••

Ask Without Pushing

••

Reflex Statement	**Articulate Alternative**
This year's vacation budget is $1,500.	I think we should have a vacation budget of $1,500 this year. What do you think?

Your bill-paying scheme is indecipherable.	Can you please tell me why it is important to you to pay all our bills on Monday mornings?
I never have any new clothes.	I am feeling a little ragtag these days. Is there any free money in the budget to buy me a new outfit or two?
I see our investments are falling through the floor.	I noticed that the FedEx stock dropped five points last week. Can we talk for a minute about whether we should sell?
I want to sell you on the idea of buying a boat.	Can we talk a bit about some of the boats I have been looking at?
I'm going to invest our money in the stock market.	I think we should invest in stocks. What do you think?
I want a bigger house.	We are really filling this house up these days. I think we should have a bigger house. How do you feel about it?

•••

Know When You Are Done

Once you have shared your opinion and made your request, understand that your initial conversational work is complete. There is nothing more to say.

Sometimes people end their portion of a talk with statements like these:

"I know this isn't really important and I'm sorry to bring it up."
"I'm sorry for being so sensitive and so afraid of the risks this
investment presents."
"In sum, I guess I want to have a credit card, although I suppose it's
not that big a deal."

These sorts of statements undermine your position. How can
you expect your partner to take you seriously if you tell her
your feelings and viewpoints are not important?

Make sure, too, that you don't leap to some horrible conclusion just because your partner sits there and fidgets for a
minute or two after you finish. If you make a statement like
"You'd say okay right away if you really loved me," you'll kill
the conversational flow at a critical time—just when your partner is thinking about what you said.

You have prepared, organized, and articulated your
thoughts, and you have avoided confrontation. As this is a relationship, it is now time to let your partner's energy carry the
exchange. After you make your request, your next step is to
listen.

A Partner's Role: Be Articulate in Response

When you are the invitee in a money discussion, you have certain responsibilities.

For example, if your mate approaches you wanting to discuss money while you are putting a new fence in the backyard
or when you are about to leave for a meeting with a new
client, you must suggest that the discussion be postponed to
a later time.

If she tells you she wants to discuss all the clothes you have
purchased recently and whether to sue the neighbors about the

damage to the driveway, request that she limit the discussion to one issue.

Once you have agreed to have the discussion, resist all urges to interrupt, leave the room, or make disparaging faces. Make yourself comfortable and accessible. Your main task is to listen, save for two small exceptions.

First, if you truly don't understand what your partner is saying, point this out for the sake of clarity and communication:

"I want to hear what you have to say, but I don't understand what money you mean when you say 'nest egg.' Do you mean the savings account, the equity we have in the house, or both?"
"Excuse me, but I must admit I don't know how a Treasury bill works. Can you please explain it to me?"

Second, if your partner says, "You have mismanaged our investments," or "Your job is making our life miserable," respond to these attacks constructively:

• Resist the urge to dismiss her concerns with "I did not" or "Too bad." Refrain from volleying back with "You're insane" or some other insulting remark of your own. Such comments will pull you into a "Yes, you did/No, I didn't" seesaw, waste your time, and wear the two of you out.

• Remind yourself that it is unlikely your partner despises you. She may feel manipulated by you or angry about some of your actions, but she probably does not intend to accuse you of massive character defects.

• Remind your partner that you would really like to know how she feels and which particular actions of yours have upset her: "I'm sorry you're upset. I can assure you that I am not managing our money with the specific intent of upsetting you.

I also assume that you are here not to attack me but to let me know that some of my actions are upsetting to you. Can you tell me specifically what upsets you?"

By helping her practice the grammar of money, you decrease the likelihood of further attacks on you, and you help guide her to articulate exactly what is troubling her. Meanwhile, you can also feel good about responding to a difficult situation with such dexterity.

When your partner seems to have finished, ask, "Is that all?" or "Does anything more come to mind?" This sort of follow-up question has several advantages. Most importantly, it will help your partner present all of his thoughts. If you haven't heard his whole viewpoint, you can't formulate a complete and meaningful response. It's like trying to react to an offer to buy your house without reading two of the pages. You need to examine the entire document before you reply.

These questions also give you some extra time to ruminate on your response, and they signal your partner that you are not so incensed about her comments that you intend to bite her head off.

••

Be Articulate in Response

••

Reflex Statement	Articulate Response
You've mismanaged our investments.	Please tell me how you feel, what you see as wrong, and specifically what you would like me to do.

You are manipulating me, and I want you to stop.	Could you please give me an example of what you are talking about and how it makes you feel?
We need to talk about the checkbook again. You are spending too much.	I don't know how to respond to that statement. Can you please tell me more specifically how you feel and what you want?
You're going to have to give up your club membership so we can make the mortgage payment.	Things must be tighter than I realized. How did you come to that conclusion?
You didn't make the cable TV payment, did you?	I didn't, and I apologize. It's my fault and I'm responsible, because I told you I would do it. I'm not trying to mess our life up. I just forgot, and I apologize for that. (Pause.) There's one thing I would like to know, if you could share it with me: why does this upset you so much?

••

From here it's your task to articulate your thoughts, and it is your partner's task to listen. Handle interruptions firmly and politely. Remember that you are only expressing your thoughts: practice money grammar, share your opinion, ask without pushing, and know when you are done. You don't have to agree. There will be time for that later on.

Set an Inspired Tone

Whether you discuss investments, budget inequities, or plans for your future, you will have many opportunities both to listen and to speak in the course of a money conversation. Here are some simple suggestions to keep in mind so that you set a tone that will enhance your communication.

REMEMBER YOUR MANNERS. Just because you two decide to talk about money does not mean your relationship goes on hold. Even if your partner never acknowledges your courtesy, he will appreciate it.

TAKE YOUR TIME. Don't rush into your response. If you need time to think about what your partner has said about how you have handled the checkbook, say so. Break for a cup of tea, perhaps. Let your full response develop before you speak. Understand that your first words may not be your response, just you thinking out loud as you formulate your response.

Note that there's no need to rush your discussion to a conclusion, either. If you need a break at a difficult moment, take one. If you think the two of you are about to become genuinely hurt over the issues, postpone the rest of the talk. After listening to her opinion of her investment plan and giving your own initial response, you may want to mull things over. If so, adjourn, and come back to the discussion the next day.

Finally, don't rush off at the end of a discussion. Go for a hug, or switch the conversation to a lighter topic. Suggest tea and a cookie, or perhaps go out for a frozen yogurt.

EXPRESS YOUR APOLOGIES. I once organized a fund-raising dinner for which the dinner committee used a wealthy woman's name on the invitation by mistake. The woman was infuriated that we used her name without her consent and phoned me to say so. Although she fully supported the dinner's beneficiary, she would not be in town to attend the dinner and she thought her absence would reflect poorly on her.

Three times this woman unleashed a torrent of fury at me, going into great detail about my thoughtlessness and her outrage. Three times I squirmed in my seat as I listened, then told her the truth: she was right, we had made a mistake, and since I was the chairperson of the committee, it was my fault, and I regretted the error deeply.

After my third apology the woman asked how preparations for the dinner were going. She then wondered how many people I expected to attend. We talked for a few minutes about these topics and about the two featured speakers. She ended our conversation by thanking me for all the work I had put into the dinner, and wishing me a pleasant evening.

Apologizing is a powerful move. It gives people permission and the opportunity to be upset. Once they express their feelings and have them acknowledged, they can leave those feelings behind and move on.

If you realize that you have insulted your partner in one of your discussions, apologize. If you have hung on to the checkbook all week and left him feeling untrustworthy, admit your mistake. Your partner may need your apology before your life together can continue.

RECOGNIZE YOUR OPTION. Remember throughout your money discussions that your every reaction is a choice you make. If your partner bounces a check because you have left too little money in the checking account, being angry at her is not a legally required or a biologically dictated response. It is certainly understandable, but it is your choice.

NAVIGATE WITH SOUL

There will be times in your relationship when you both express yourselves on a financial issue and the appropriate course of action will be easy to identify.

"I want to switch banks because those people treat me as if I'm stupid and untalented when I walk in with Tommy or without a suit on."—"Changing banks seems like the right move to me."

"I think we should pay Louise an extra $15 a week because a trustworthy cleaning person is hard to find and I don't want to lose her."—"I wouldn't want to either. Let's do it."

"We both need to be doing work that develops our talents and yields satisfaction as well as a good income. Let's figure out how you can start a graphic design firm and how I can get into that master's program."—"That sounds great."

At other times, however, your view will not match your partner's and neither of you will be eager to compromise. Should you put your money in a mutual fund? Does he deserve more new clothes than you because he works downtown and you don't? Should you sell the house you inherited or rent it?

You can debate such questions all day long and never resolve them. There are no magic words that can force someone to change his or her opinion. More importantly, there are no right answers to these questions. Nothing about a mutual fund will make it good under all circumstances. Nothing about owning real estate will ensure happiness for both of you. Saving for retirement has been recommended by every conference of financial planners since Caesar ruled Rome, but if saving for retirement interferes with the two of you creating a fulfilling life together, it is advice of the most useless sort.

If you insist on debating what you think about these questions, you typically wind up in one of the loops described at the outset of the chapter—combat, retreat, or exile. When that happens, your money talks tend to be painful rather than pleasant. Some of this is because of the arguing, and some of it is because discussions focusing on mortgage rates, shopping sprees, or credit ratings have nothing to do with your talent, spirit, vision, or the way you want to grow as individuals and as a couple.

In addition, when you confine yourselves to discussing houses, clothes, and mutual funds, your satisfaction with your money decisions tends to be a hit-or-miss proposition, because even when you agree on such issues, that is not much to build a life on.

How do you avoid all these problems? You have to look beyond the immediate issues, your immediate point of view, and the math of personal finance. You have to realize that your opinion of a particular financial issue is not necessarily what you want from life. You need a deeper connection.

Instead of debating financial issues, focus on knowing the answers to these essential questions:

THE SOUL-TO-SOUL QUESTIONS

- What work do you both want to do to bring your talents forth?
- How do you like to take care of yourself—exercising or yoga, perhaps?
- How do you like to take care of each other—by making breakfast or taking the children out on Saturday mornings so Mom can sleep in?
- What sort of church life or spiritual life do you want?

- What activities are healthy and nourishing for your children and your whole family?
- What's good for your romance? Baby-sitting, overnight trips, and getting home in time to enjoy a relaxed dinner together are possibilities.
- What makes life simpler and less burdensome? A cleaning person, perhaps, or having both parents home in the evening.
- What do you want out of this relationship? Family, sincerity, companionship? You fill in the blank.
- What are you here to do?

The point here is to ask yourselves what is important to you in a timeless and enduring way. These questions will help you loosen your grip on the financial issues of the moment. The answers to these larger questions are the signposts that will point you toward money decisions that will help you grow into a great life together, decisions that will yield both tangible and intangible rewards.

One evening Nancy told me that the dance studio where she took classes was increasing its fees by $45 a month because attendance was down. At that time, our coffers were not flush with cash, but she naturally wanted to continue taking the class because she loves to dance.

My first thought translated roughly into this: Man, these guys don't know what they're doing. They can't run their club efficiently, and we can't afford to pay for their ineptitude. We cannot just fork over another $600 a year just because they can't pull bodies through the door.

Fortunately I did not actually say this. Instead, I gave myself an extra moment to have a second thought. That one translated roughly into this: This is Nancy asking for this. Working out makes her happy about herself physically; it boosts her self-esteem. She is good at it, it expresses her spirit, and it adds dimension to her life. It is a healthy counterpoint to her work as a writer. It makes her a happier person in a way that nothing else can. This is a no-brainer. We have to figure out how to swing it.

I then told Nancy, "Well, let's just figure out how to swing it."

The next time you and your partner discuss a financial issue and you find yourself in disagreement, move to the soul-to-soul questions. See if the answers to those questions direct you toward a decision that will enhance your relationship. As was the case for me, you may discover that while you have differences, you have no differences of substance.

When Pauline and Doug disagreed on how to proceed on a real estate deal, they used the questions to reach a similarly satisfying result. After one round of counteroffers, the buyer had come up to $138,000, and Pauline and Doug needed to respond. Doug wanted to ask for $143,000, while Pauline just wanted to accept the buyer's latest counter.

Doug was sure the buyer would accept whatever they proposed. His wife was concerned about losing the buyer and then having to split the family apart. She had already wound down her photography work and could move any time, but Doug had to leave for a new job in Atlanta in six weeks. If the house was not sold by then, Pauline and their son, Austin, would have to stay behind to complete the sale.

After some discussion the couple decided to sell the house for $138,000. Why did Doug relent? Because he basically wanted the same things Pauline did. He wanted his family together, and he wanted his wife to be able to settle into new surroundings and resume her work. By looking beyond the numbers, they found common ground and let that common vision dictate their decision.

It turned out that giving up the $5,000 not only worked for their life together but also yielded some very bankable benefits. The buyer had no obligation to agree. He could have walked away from the deal, and the house could easily have sat on the market for another three months. During this time Doug and Pauline would have had to pay a mortgage in California plus a rental payment in Atlanta, as well as airfare to see each other. They also would have had to do without Pauline's income for that period. These items could easily have amounted to well over $5,000.

Using the soul-to-soul questions to make financial decisions as a couple may sound like an expensive way to live. Like Doug and Pauline, however, you and your partner will discover that what's good for your relationship is often good for your net worth as well.

CREATE A FULL FUTURE TOGETHER: BE ARTICULATE

When you follow the steps for being articulate about money, you gain a new perspective on all sorts of financial issues, from how much to leave in the checking account to how much to spend on a house. With this perspective, it's easier to identify steps that will keep you two in sync and lead to a fulfilling life together. The inevitable differences of financial opinion will become easier to overlook or to give up when you have something larger to live for.

By contrast, if you ignore these steps and insist on debating the beauty of your own viewpoint in a money discussion with your partner, you may never get around to addressing the soul-to-soul questions. Instead, you may collapse what you think about financial issues into what you truly want out of life. This will squeeze the spirit right out of both your discussions and your life. It will also keep you from putting your funds to work creating the life the two of you could have.

In Chapter 7 we will see how, with one slight adjustment, these three basic steps for talking about money—setting up a connection, expressing yourself, and navigating with soul—will also work well in negotiating with others and insinuating yourself in the marketplace. For now we turn to understanding unspoken communications with money, which is just as critical to fulfilling your promise as learning how to talk about it.

PRACTICE

1. Practice listening. One place to start is during "how was your day" discussions over dinner. Practice being entirely silent while your partner speaks. Ask her a question that will help her expand her point or draw her out.

2. Make a list of your soul-to-soul questions—what's important to you in life and what you perceive to be important to the two of you in your life together. Include thoughts on the talents you have, the ones you would like to develop, and the ones your partner has. Have a separate paragraph that lists four things you thought were important in life and have found you can do without. Discuss your lists together with your partner.

3. Recall a recent money discussion with your partner. When did you talk? What was the topic? Was the issue resolved to your satisfaction and your partner's?

4. Recall a money discussion that would have ended differ-

ently had you focused more on the soul-to-soul questions. Recall one that worked out well because you based your actions on these essential issues. Note both the personal and the financial consequences of your decisions.

5. What two financial issues would you like to discuss with your partner? Follow the steps outlined in this chapter and have the discussions. Note how they go, and decide what adjustments you can make in conversation mechanics that will make your discussions more pleasant and more fruitful.

6. Can you see the application of this chapter to your discussions with third parties, such as your stockbroker, someone who is going to buy your house, or your decision to take a certain job?

Circuit Training

1. How are your dates going?

2. Name ten things you are great at. Name ten things you wish you were great at. Name ten things your partner is great at.

3. Do the two of you get enough sleep at night? Are you able to fit in an occasional nap? How could you arrange to get more rest this month?

4. Is there a particular time when working out feels best to you? If you find yourself getting a bit stale, move your workout to a different time slot. Consider exercising early in the morning, when the boost from the workout can carry you through the day.

3 The Rewards of
Being Aware

When Jake left his job and steady salary at the hospital to start his own physical therapy practice, he was concerned about Ellen. Their relationship had been wonderful up until that point, and he did not want that to change. At the time their boys were nine and four, and Ellen was doing an occasional graphic design assignment. He knew there would be very little spare cash for a while.

Jake was sure that he was reading the market correctly, that Ellen would be a great graphic designer, and that their cash flow would improve in time. Meanwhile he did not want her to feel discouraged because he had to work so much or because vacations were so infrequent. He did not want her to think she had to give up designing to take a job that paid more but that would force her to put her passion on hold.

He developed the habit of putting an extra five- or ten-dollar bill on Ellen's purse occasionally. That way, he figured, she wouldn't have to stop at the bank if she wanted a bagel or needed some gas, and her day would be a bit easier. Ellen appreciated knowing that he was thinking about her.

Ellen developed the habit of always making time to listen to Jake as he talked through his ideas for his practice. Her perspective and support, especially when he felt discouraged, were essential to his success.

Today both Jake's practice and Ellen's designing have grown, their cash flow is much greater, and their life together continues to be a happy one. You could say that they have thrived because he has talent, because Ellen is a rare woman, or because they are committed to each other. All of this is true, yet they needed more than that to build their life day by day. One of the key reasons that Jake and Ellen could take the risks they did and emerge with life better than ever was that they excelled at being aware of the messages they transmitted with money.

We all transmit three sorts of very explicit messages as we act with and around money. We exchange these unspoken messages with our partners. We exchange them with others as we transact in the marketplace. We also direct a steady stream of these messages to ourselves.

Being aware of these messages is money's second fundamental practice. When you and your partner fail to log on to this fiscal frequency, you tend to create situations in which your relationship, your self-esteem, your connection with others, and your wallet sustain major injuries. By developing an awareness of money messages, you can eliminate a lot of the negative waves flowing through your house and your head, and fashion a more nourishing life together. You can also avoid circumstances that are likely to cause you financial trauma, and you can move more directly toward large material rewards.

MESSAGES BETWEEN PARTNERS

One afternoon Pam bought some clothes at Banana Republic. That evening she showed them to Ray, who told her that they could not afford the expense. The following day she returned the outfits. Two weeks later Ray brought home a new suit, never mentioning it to his wife.

Ray told himself that he needed to look impressive to the people at headquarters when he traveled to New York later that month. He might as well have told Pam, "Your name is on the checks, but the money in the account is mine."

When Theresa married John he owned a stock portfolio worth close to $150,000 and she was a nurse with an interest in photography. She signed the prenuptial agreement and the budget he insisted on, thinking that these documents would not really influence their marriage. Over time, however, her thinking has changed. Theresa believes their life would be much easier in a house instead of a condo, but John steadfastly refuses to consider selling any stock to finance the move. He also resists the idea of cashing in some securities to help her start a photography business.

When these topics come up, he tells Theresa, "We have an agreement and we need to stick to it." To Theresa this sounds more like "Take my wife—I need my money."

Andrew earns a handsome income working in the marketing department of a software company. He also averages about sixty hours a week at the office and regularly travels around the country on business. He wants a less demanding job, but he knows that this would almost certainly mean a cut in pay. He is also aware that Jessica does not want to give up the Bahamian vacations and the BMW she has become so accustomed to.

Jessica told Andrew he would be "wimping out" if he eased up on the corporate climb at this point. She might as well have come out and said, "I don't care how you feel—just bring home my bucks."

ACT LIKE A PARTNER, NOT A TYCOON

The most devastating money messages flowing between partners arise from the behavior connected with two basic issues. The first of these is this: whose money is it to spend—mine or ours?

Jessica's actions left the impression that her love had rather narrow limits, that she had a private agenda, and that life with her was cold. John and Ray left the same impression with their partners. All three used money in a way that telegraphed the message: "I love my money more than I love you."

How do you keep such messages from working their way into your relationship? If you are serious about building a life together, you need to act like a partner, not a tycoon. You must make a constant conscious effort to act in a way that expresses a different attitude: "The money belongs to both of us."

A certain author, you may feel, has just lost radio contact with reality. Perhaps you inherited control of your father's real estate holdings. Perhaps you came to your relationship with a pile of cash or you earn thousands more than your partner every month. Maybe you take pride in your independent streak, or perhaps you are used to being taken care of. On the surface it may appear to you that your partner has no connection whatsoever to funds you regard as yours. Why shouldn't these be yours and yours alone to control?

The answer is that, if you want to rid your house of divisive money messages, you don't have a choice. A mine-yours division of finance forces you into actions that carry a message of separation rather than one of togetherness. The mine-yours split leads you to police expenses, defend expenses, debate contributions, reconcile accounts, overlook feelings, squirrel away assets, grapple for control of bargaining sessions, and chaperon independent investments. This is fine work if you run a pension fund for a pipe fitters union, but it's a poor way to negotiate a marriage of the spirit.

These actions say hold back instead of bring forth. They say dictate instead of collaborate. You may be married according to the laws of the state, but these actions say you are not really engaged.

If you behave this way, the distressing dispatches will continue, you will regularly alienate your love and deflate her affection, and emotional stab wounds will be almost inevitable. You may acquire the clothes, the car, the financial guarantees, or the investment control you seek, and you and your partner may even stay together forever. Your experience, however, will be a limited partnership at best.

The opportunity before you in being together, remember, is to coauthor a story that has never been told before. Either you're in on the writing or you're out. If you really want to share your life, you need to expand your focus beyond your cash.

Guidelines for Genuine Partnership

Conveying a "these-funds-belong-to-both-of-us" attitude entails three tasks. One task is to work on simply becoming aware of the nonverbal messages you telegraph. What are you saying to your love with the way you handle the checkbook, the bills, the mutual fund updates, or the cash? Slow down and observe your actions. Think about what they speak.

If you forget to consider this in advance, think about it afterward.

The other two tasks are to modify your behavior where necessary so as to convey the "this-is-ours" sentiments you intend, and to supplement these signals with ample talk about your life together. Be energetic and inventive here. Leave a ten-dollar bill on your partner's wallet so he has money to buy lunch today. Ask him if he has the clothes he needs for the coming season. Resist the inquisition-like urge to ask about the cost of the groceries he bought or the leather basketball he brought home for your daughters.

Invite her to tell you whether she is happy about how you two are handling the sale of your house or the investment of your savings. Volunteer that you have no problem taking a less glitzy vacation this year, given the unexpected cost of removing the two dead trees in the side yard.

When she tells you she wants to quit her job, don't automatically blurt out, "But we need the money!" Instead of waiting for her to ask for a new car, propose that you buy her one. If you realize you have just barged into her discussion with a difficult salesperson, apologize and stand back.

Don't let your fears dissuade you from saying, "I love you," with your money. Remember that self-esteem and security are not a function of how much you have stashed in a private account. They are the direct result of valuing and developing your talents.

DOES TAKING THIS IT'S-ALL-OURS APPROACH MEAN I CAN NEVER DO ANYTHING WITH MONEY WITHOUT CONSULTING MY PARTNER? There's no need to feel paralyzed. Simply pause to consider the impact of your actions. Be thoughtful.

Sometimes you will want to consult your partner where you sense a negative message could be conveyed. If you don't confer with her in these cases, remember to let her know what you have done with your funds soon after the event. She may be hurt that you bought a new CD player for your car at a time when cash flow seemed tight to her, but your rapport will take an even bigger hit if she finds out from the credit card bill instead of from you.

Checking your messages may feel awkward at first. In time it will simply become a habit that keeps you in sync with someone you love.

DOES TAKING A PARTNERSHIP APPROACH TO OUR FUNDS MEAN THAT WE MUST POOL ALL OUR ACCOUNTS? Not at all.

Ellen owned some stocks and an IRA when she married Jake. He also owned an IRA as well as an interest in an apartment house. They have never changed formal ownership of any of these assets, except for pulling some money out of both IRAs to fund Jake's new firm and Ellen's designing. They have separate checking accounts for their businesses and a joint checking and savings account for the household. They reason that if they need the money that's invested in the IRAs, the stocks, or the apartment house, they will sell those assets and use it, but meanwhile, for the sake of convenience, they leave it where it is.

Pooling your every last cent just because you are together is just as artificial as keeping all your money separate. As long as you both consider the money to be on call for your life together, you can keep it wherever you want to.

WHAT IF HE SPENDS HIS WAY THROUGH OUR MONEY? This is a common fear, but barricading your money in a separate account is not the answer. If your partner's actions scare you, talk to him using the guidelines from the previous chapter. Go over the soul-to-soul questions, acquire some sense of the life you two are aiming for, and pursue that vision. This course, not separate accounts, will create the bright future you seek.

If your partner will not talk about these topics with you and collaborate on a life you two envision, understand that this is a signal that your relationship has a very limited arc. In such cases the impulse is often to think that you need heightened security for your funds. Perhaps what you really need is a new partner.

WHAT IF SHE MARRIES ME SO SHE CAN RUN OFF WITH MY MONEY? WHAT IF HE LEAVES AFTER I HAVE INVESTED ALL OF THIS MONEY IN HIM? If you harbor this reservation, you may want to spend more time asking yourself exactly why you are marrying this person in the first place. The relationship might well go further if you two develop a bit more trust—not a better prenuptial agreement—before the ceremony.

The irony of any division of finance—from a prenuptial contract or an equity-sharing real estate arrangement to a simple agreement to split expenses—is that no matter how much effort and money you invest in trying to contrive a deal that apportions assets and obligations fairly between you, it is impossible to perform the operation successfully.

"This money is my money, not yours," you may say. Yet it is naive to think that the problems you experience in investing it or earning it will not be discussed over dinner or during evening walks and that his support and counsel will not be instrumental in your success with those tasks. How do you reward him fairly for such contributions?

This is 80 percent my home, you may say, because I put up the down payment and I pay half of the monthly mortgage. Suppose the market drops 20 percent, she bails you out of five mortgage payments because you lose your job, and she helps you build a new den. What's her share worth then?

That bill is your problem, not mine, you may say. Yet his anxieties will surely affect your rapport and how you handle your funds. How much does his trouble really end up costing you?

If you are not yet prepared for a full commitment to each other, don't rush into trying to meld your lives and your finances. Trying to put your bodies together while processing billboard-sized messages that you still want to be apart will exhaust you. It will snuff out the spark you feel for each other.

When you are ready to build a life together, however, build it. Don't hold back. Stock the atmosphere with the healthiest money messages possible. Replenish regularly. Rather than immobilizing yourself with the constant calculation of who owns how much of what, pour yourself into creating the richest possible rapport you can muster.

···

ACT LIKE A PARTNER, NOT A TYCOON

The Tycoon Lifestyle

···

Routine Transmission	**Message Received**
Your adjustable-rate mortgage rises a quarter point, and you remind your partner that you could have qualified for a fixed-rate loan at a lower rate if only she earned more money.	You are standing there, but all I see is your income.
Your partner is asking your broker a question, and you	You are tiresome and inept.

interrupt her in midquery with,
"No, no, no, no, no, Janine—
listen to me."

You commandeer the finances and try to make up for it with lots of gifts.	We can't afford to have you handle this. Sit there and I'll do it.
You have the last word on all family investment decisions.	I call the shots here.
You control the family's only credit card.	I don't trust you to make those kinds of decisions.
You insist on checking her math when she leaves a tip.	Yes, yes, I love you, but the money steals my heart.
When he suggests you vacation for ten days instead of just five, you veto the idea. You then buy yourself a new Toyota.	I love what the money does for me.
You let a check bounce because he did not deposit his paycheck on time.	My love for you ends at this line here.

••

Genuine Partnership

••

Routine Transmission	**Message Received**
You pay off your husband's credit cards when you get married.	We're in this life together.

You give your boyfriend an extra $100 a month so he can rent his own apartment and your relationship can proceed without interference from his boorish roommate.	I want to see where we can go.
Seeing what good the physical therapy does her after elbow surgery, you suggest that she arrange for some extra appointments, even though the health insurance will not cover any more visits and you'll have to pull the money out of the retirement fund.	Let's get you healthy, and then we'll figure out how to earn more money.
You let your wife buy the swing set that she wants to buy for your son.	I'm willing to share the steering wheel with you.
You use the checkbook jointly and make a conscious effort not to criticize his every expenditure.	I love you.
Knowing that cash flow is tight, you propose to pay some bills out of your separate account.	We're into this love together.
When your partner tells you that the cash flow looks tight this month and asks you to pay three bills out of your separate account, you respond, "No problem."	This love is a joint effort.

Once cash flow resumes, you make a point of putting some money back into her account, and you say thank you for the money she spent on bills.

This love is a joint effort.

The two of you talk about having a light Christmas spending season, and you implement your plan without subsequently complaining about it.

I'm with you stride for stride.

You see her workout leotards are fraying, so you suggest she buy some new ones.

I love you.

....

TAKE A STAKE IN HER

How important is your partner's work to you? This is the other issue that gives rise to money messages that can sour your romance.

Kirk's annual sales projection report was taking much longer to complete than he had anticipated. He really wanted it finished by Friday and couldn't tell how much longer it would take. From his point of view, there was only one thing to do.

He phoned Megan and told her, "I've got to work, so I won't be able to take care of Natalie this evening. I'm sorry, but you'll have to miss your filmmaking class again."

Kirk's behavior discounts Megan's talent and undermines

her self-esteem. He essentially employs money to dispatch a cutting message: "You are just not that valuable to me."

How do you keep this signal from surfacing in your relationship? You need to take a stake in your partner. You need to act with the specific purpose of communicating a different message: "I'm just as interested in the development of your talents as I am in the development of mine."

It's easy to pay lip service to your interest in your love and then to gloss right over the real work of making the investment. Maybe your partner thinks he does not want to work, so you feel that lets you off the hook. Maybe you earn the money that makes the household go, so you feel there is financial justification for giving your work priority at all times. Perhaps your partner has never specifically complained about how you treat his work.

At first glance it may seem that your partner's work is just a midlevel issue at best. What's in it for you? Why bother to give his work just as much support as your own?

One simple reason: to grow together, you both need to grow. If your actions say that her talents are not worth developing, you will help kill her belief in herself and inhibit her growth as a person. In the short term your message will cause resentment. In the long term—if there is one—acting like a bystander in your partner's life will produce a lopsided relationship.

Project ahead a decade or two. You will have patients or clients to see, perhaps articles to write and conventions to attend. Maybe you will switch fields completely, so you will have a challenging new mountain to climb. By nurturing your work, you will have interesting ways to connect with people and to bolster your self-esteem.

Think about how gritty your life will taste, however, if your partner does not do the same. Perhaps she will be basically doing the same job she did twenty years earlier. Perhaps she will not work at all, but instead will cook dinner, run the vegetable garden and the dog, and take care of birthdays, holidays, and your taxes. How strong a bond will you share at that point? What dreams of hers will have been stifled? Who will she blame for this?

Look around. Plenty of couples have gone down this path. You may have grown up in a household where one partner received virtually no support for the development of her talents, but you cannot afford to make the same mistake. The stakes are too great. Letting her pick out the furniture will not be enough to keep you close. You need to back her up.

Sometimes we only need one person to believe in us in order to do great things, fulfill our potential as human beings, and feel good about ourselves. Be that person for your partner.

Guidelines for Taking a Stake

Taking a stake in your partner's work involves the same three steps as acting like a partner with your money: think about it, talk about it, and do it.

Check the nonverbal messages you telegraph. What are you saying to your love with the way you schedule meetings, divide household chores, or plan vacations? Are you oblivious to her needs, a mere spectator in her work life?

Do you spend time talking about his work as well as yours? Are you in the habit of investing comparable amounts of money in both your careers? Do you talk about what she needs to do to feel good about herself? Slow down and observe your actions. Think about what they say.

In conjunction with observing yourself more closely, take a spirited and imaginative role in backing your partner's work life. Volunteer to take the children for the morning so she can catch up on her designing. Pick up a course catalog for the degree she has mused about working toward. Pick up the dry cleaning.

Make some calls and look around the neighborhood to see if you can find him a quieter office. Ask if he likes his work. Applaud his attempts to moonlight or to learn about different work, even if you think it will be years before his efforts produce any income.

When she tells you she wants to quit her job, don't automatically blurt out, "But you can't do anything else!" If she's not comfortable with baby-sitters yet, come home at noon once a week so she will have at least a little time to stay in touch with her practice. As the children settle into school or into lives of their own, ask her what kind of work she thinks she can do and what she needs to begin doing it.

Tell her, "We have $4,000 to get you started," and tell her you believe she can do it.

Remember it is not your place to weigh the merit of your partner's course. If he wants to write poetry, you need to help him write. If she wants to design bicycles, you need to help her design. Your task is to champion your partner's work simply because it's your partner's. If he stumbles, your task is to help him regain his stride. Your message must be absolute: no matter what she needs, you will help her obtain it; no matter whether she succeeds or fails, you will be right there in her corner.

In gauging how much help you can give, do not be overly realistic. It's easy to reason that you have to take care of your job, that there are only so many hours in the day, or that you have a finite amount of cash. This is all true, but too often when we are realistic we sell ourselves—or someone we love—short. Do all you can, no more and no less.

In the short term the payoff may be purely intangible. Withhold judgment. You have no idea when that journal will turn into a book that will sell a staggering number of copies. You have no idea when all those hours in that makeshift workshop will yield a two-wheeled idea around which a whole company can be built. You also have no idea when the income differential in your house will undergo a radical reversal. If you are earning the lesser amount in the future, you will still want to have your work accorded respect.

Invest your effort and your funds to create a fertile environment, and be willing to wait for the return. The richest life together is never a linear experience.

••

TAKE A STAKE IN HER

The Bystander Lifestyle

••

Routine Transmission	Message Received
You leave life's valet work—picking up dry cleaning, chauffeuring the children, purchasing birthday gifts, buying groceries, housecleaning—to your partner.	I have the real job.
Your partner misses out on an assignment because you set up	You just aren't that important.

the vacation without taking her
schedule as a freelancer into
consideration.

You pour your money into
savings, new video equipment,
and a beach house, all the while
knowing your partner is working
at a job he finds far less than
fulfilling.

You don't really matter.

As your partner works on
producing an independent film,
you tell her a story about an
independent filmmaker who
went bankrupt.

You can't do what you have
in mind.

You indeed believe that your
husband is talented,
but he has no work and you do
nothing about it.

It doesn't matter to me what
you do.

Your wife floats the idea of
working toward a master's
degree in education, and you
opine that it would ruin your
summer.

You aren't that important.

Your partner wants to quit his
job. You say, "To do what?
That's all you know."

Others can flourish, but I doubt
that you can.

Your partner wants to work
part-time, and you tell her that
whatever she earns would be
eaten up by preschool and
office costs.

The development of your talent
is worth nothing to me.

| You give him all the money he needs and the freedom to do what he wants, but you never attend any of his watercolor shows. | You are valuable to me, but not so much that I'd invest anything important. |

•••

Backing Your Partner

•••

Routine Transmission	**Message Received**
Knowing that your partner's job depresses her, you propose that she find different work, quitting her job if she has to and tapping your savings if you must.	I am interested in you.
Having heard your partner talk about all the writing she did in college, you propose that she take the checkbook and sign up for a course in writing short stories.	I think you'd be good at it.
You have your car phone disconnected, knowing that if she wants to write, she'll need a small office and the rent will have to come from somewhere.	I am fully invested in your life.
"If you need to catch up on your work on Sunday, I will take Emily to the zoo."	You can count on me.
You clear all your stuff out of the desk in the den and tell her	In my mind, the possibilities are excellent.

it's her space for drawing all the comic strips she wants.

You get the children off to school twice a week and cook dinner three nights a week.	You matter.
You acknowledge her taking on the extra burden of doing all the cooking for a week without complaint, knowing you had key meetings about your new firm.	Thank you for the sacrifices you make for me.
You do all the cooking the following week, knowing that your partner just did this for you last week.	Let's not overlook you and your dreams.
You listen to your partner talk about her plans for her media consulting business over and over and over again.	You can do it. I know you can.
You talk about the future in terms of "When your firm grows," not "if it grows."	Your future looks bright, and I'm lucky to have found you.
Burt and Monica don't treat your wife's painting with much respect. The next time they invite you to dinner, you decline.	I will take your painting over her fricassee any day.

• •

MESSAGES IN THE MARKETPLACE

The second set of money messages you and your partner need to tune in to are the ones coming at you from other people in the marketplace. All these folks say that the work, the investment, or the negotiating proposal they offer will serve you. Many claim to be easy to deal with. How do you tell the good opportunities from the ones to avoid? You need to become advanced students of people's behavior with money. Embedded in a person's words and her actions are signals that will tell you whether your experience with her will be a profitable one.

Which behavior patterns do you study? Unfortunately, many people zero in on the wrong cues. The quality of someone's office space, clothes, cars, and letterhead will tell you little of import about him. Important-sounding titles, diplomas from prestigious schools, and large stock portfolios do not reveal what you want to know. There is less to expensive accessories than meets the eye.

To build your bankbook and move smoothly forward with your life, you and your partner must have the discipline to look past all this makeup. You need to deal with people who have the motivation and competence to respect your time and talent, present you with straightforward propositions, and keep their promises. Three steps will help you flourish in the marketplace.

DEAL WITH PEOPLE WHO
CAN PART WITH THEIR FUNDS

A number of years ago an apparently wealthy orthopedic surgeon hired me to help him arrange a real estate transaction.
During our initial discussion we talked about the property he
owned, the buyer, and the sales terms he hoped to achieve. I
also learned that he was suing a car dealer for selling him a
Lincoln with a supposedly defective engine, and he needed the
name of a good real estate litigator so he could sue a pair of
brokers because he felt they had coerced him into selling an
office building too cheaply two years earlier. He asked to pay
half of my retainer in thirty days, a request I denied.

As negotiations with the buyer commenced, communications with the surgeon were strained. At one point he told me
that he could probably agree to terms more easily "if you
wanted to throw in some of your fee." As we checked our cal-
endars to set up a meeting with the buyer, he remarked, "For
what I'm paying you, you should be available twenty-four
hours a day." When I tried to curtail one of his rambling telephone monologues by reminding him that I wanted to keep his
bill to a minimum, he replied, "You're not advising me here—
we're just talking. There's no charge for talking."

With that remark all the signals he had flashed at me suddenly made sense—the doc was a walking collection problem.
That afternoon I sent him an invoice for the $1,668 he owed me
for services to date. Predictably, he telephoned with an ambulance full of reasons why, retainer agreement notwithstanding,
he owed me absolutely nothing.

I decided to end our relationship on the spot, before the
aggravation or the accounts payable piled up any further. This

was not easy, as the doctor had a backup ambulance full of reasons why I was legally required to continue representing him. None of these was legitimate, but I still triple-checked all the paperwork as I removed myself from the case, quite aware that he might launch one of his lawsuits in my direction.

At the time, I considered the doctor one of those special people I would like to have seen on the business end of a Stephen King novel, and yet a good chunk of the blame for my predicament rested with me.

The doctor told me right in the middle of our first meeting that he had difficulty letting money leave his grasp—he tried to avoid paying my retainer. I failed to see the signal.

He also let me know the extent to which his closefisted nature dominated his life—he described his variety pack of lawsuits in great detail. Again the signal sailed past me unrecognized.

I was preoccupied with the thought that I could earn some money and possibly some referrals to well-off clients. This error cost me about $2,500 and several long stretches of elevated blood pressure. It also cost Nancy and me time we spent helping me vent my frustration over this client, time we could have spent talking about her latest short story or playing with Amanda.

I did my best to put the mess with the doctor behind me as swiftly as I could, but the lesson was not quite over. About six months after parting company with him, I stopped by the office of a friend who practices bankruptcy law. Her secretary told me she was with a client. Who emerged with my friend when the meeting ended? Bingo. In addition to telling me that he had a manic attachment to his dollars, the good doctor had been telling me that he was broke.

The marketplace is a sea of uncertain opportunities, unfamiliar faces, and great risk. At stake with each job, investment, and negotiation you undertake are your efforts, your time, and your dollars. How can you and your partner avoid troublesome and costly encounters and string together some fruitful experiences? Look for signs that people have cash to spend and that they know how to let go of it gracefully.

Many people propose to negotiate, invest, or work with you, and in the same moment indicate that they lack the motivation or the wherewithal—or perhaps both—to complete your transaction smoothly, if at all. Whether you are selling a division of IBM or looking for part-time work as a cartoonist, the signals tend to be the same.

These folks grouse about the cost of running their businesses while interviewing you for a job. They complain about how expensive your services are before they hire you. They tend to know lots of stories about how they were pirated out of this investment return or that real estate windfall.

If you misquote your investment deal by mistake, they attempt to hold you to your word. If you request a deposit on an apartment lease or a property sale, they insist on getting interest on it. If they are to let some of their hard-earned cash out of their wallets, they want a discount, a miracle, and a guarantee, and they usually want it now.

People typically clamp onto their cash like this for any one of a handful of reasons:

1. They may not really have the money to hire you.

2. They may have only a marginal interest in doing your deal.

3. They may not have figured out that they cannot secure what they want without letting go of their dollars.

4. They may believe that fiscal tightness is a standard human trait, like ears or toes.

5. They may have indexed their self-worth to their bank balance.

Regardless of which explanation applies, the message you need to be aware of is the same: I don't let my dollars out of my wallet.

Guidelines for Avoiding Tightwads

When you encounter someone who seems to have trouble parting with her funds, flesh out the message. Inquire very specifically about her motivation and bank balance. If you have yet to begin your dealings with her, be extremely plain. Estimate the total cost of your services, add 10 to 20 percent, and ask if she can accept and afford the bill if it runs that high. Discuss the downside of your investment frankly and find out if she can withstand this. Ask this person who wants to hire you about the finances and the vision for her company and how you fit into the picture.

If you are already involved with this person, obtain a sense of what the future holds. Send an invoice and see if he pays it. Ask whether he is happy with the investment or would prefer to back out. Ask if your work fits into the company's future. Ask if he has really lost interest in this particular real estate deal.

The idea here is not to make such inquiries in a way that challenges her financial machismo or bludgeons her into pressing on with you. On the contrary, the idea is to be quite nice so you can quickly obtain an unvarnished reading about her interest and intent before dealing with her costs you extra time and money.

If what you hear does not convince you that this person really has the dollars and the desire to move forward with you, find the exit. End your relationship with this client. Start looking for a different place to work. Offer to give his investment money back. Terminate the deal and find a new buyer for your house. Your life will not work if this person is bolted to the currency.

Moving on may seem like a hardship. Find a way to move on anyway. All too often we talk ourselves into dealing with people who, at the end of the day, really do not want to pay us. Well, I'm sure she'll pay eventually, we think. I can't let this opportunity pass—I need the money. I can't imagine that a man that rich wouldn't close this deal. I'm sure a person of her position won't really be that difficult an investor.

Be stronger of mind than this.

These folks will simply back out of a deal, oblivious to the inconvenience and expense they have caused you. The paychecks they are supposed to give you by the tenth will not arrive until the last week of the month. They will want the investment return they want, not just the one you earned them. They will also try to chisel you. When I presented one woman with a $4,200 invoice for my services—and bear in mind her net worth exceeded $2 million—she said, "What if I pay you $2,500 and we call it even?"

If you try to reason the tightfisted set into relaxing their grip, you will be drawn into their fixation on the dollars. This will be distracting and depressing for you. You will have to spend an inordinate amount of time jousting about invoices, phoning about paychecks, debating payment policies that you think are fair, or arguing over when the deposit was supposed to go into escrow. Mired in this money-as-commodity mud wrestling, the work you want to do will suffer. Even though you and your partner may intend to live a large life, these actions will pull you into a small place. This you can do without.

These people are not wicked human beings. Most times they are unaware that they waste your time and talent and disrupt their own lives with their actions. Your task is not to sermonize to them about how to use money. It is simply to identify them and decline to deal with them. This will leave room in your life for far more interesting connections.

**HOW CAN I RECOGNIZE THE FOLKS WITH THE MOTIVA-
TION AND THE CAPITAL TO DEAL WITH ME?** These folks can let go of their funds easily. I don't mean that they overpay, or that they squander their money on Lamborghinis. I mean that they exhibit a sense of freedom in the act of moving money to people they deal with. They move their dollars crisply.

If this type of person wants to retain your services, she typically has her checkbook handy, pays you without being reminded to do so, and smiles about it. If she wants to buy your house, she offers a suitably large deposit and offers to put it into escrow promptly.

When he proposes that you invest with him, you notice that his proposal pays investors generously and early. When he decides to invest with you, he calls to ask if he can send you his investment funds today.

These folks are not daft. They simply understand that more is afoot than mere numbers, both for them and for you. They have families to raise, lives to live, work to do, just as you and your partner do. If your deal, investment, or work suits their purposes, they want it to proceed smoothly for all concerned, and then they want to move on. They know you need to be paid, and they want that to happen so that you will remain fully motivated to complete your part of whatever bargain you have made. These people are not rich uncles. They simply see that the power in money lies in making the dollars flow, not in locking them into a wallet.

The future with these folks typically unfolds without gratuitous anxiety, bickering, or sudden surprises. They treat you fairly when they employ you or take you on as an investor. They pay you on time, and if you handle your end skillfully, they often want to work with you again.

If there are surprises, they tend to be enjoyable ones. I am thinking here of three clients who were each quite quick to put a check on my desk when they retained me. One paid me in full a month before my work was complete. Another sent me an eloquent letter of thanks with a gift certificate from a classy Italian restaurant. The third wrote a short note with a $2,000 tip in it.

When you notice that someone has a relaxed and powerful grip on her funds, put extra effort into figuring out a way to work, negotiate, or invest with her. If you are looking for some financial momentum, this is the sort of person you and your partner need to have around you.

. . . .

DEAL WITH PEOPLE WHO CAN PART WITH THEIR FUNDS

The Tightwads

. . . .

Routine Transmission	Translation
Your boss leaves the firm, and management gives you her	We don't care about you. We just want the job done.

responsibilities without pro-
moting you or giving you
a raise.

A customer pays you three weeks late without explanation.	You don't matter to me.
A client wants extra work for your standard fee.	You are not worth what you charge.
One of the prospects you approach wants a guaranteed return on the investment partnership you are setting up.	I don't really want to invest.
A couple offers to buy your house for 15 percent below your asking price.	We'll buy the home if you feel you made a foolish error in pricing it.
The boss tells you, "I won't give you a raise because I can get people to work here for less than what I'm already paying you."	You are not valuable to me.

•••

People You Can Deal With

•••

Routine Transmission	**Translation**
"I don't have the money to pay you now, but I will have it by next Thursday." The check arrives, and includes a 3 percent overage for being late.	I respect you and our relationship.

You are paid on time, in person, and with a smile.	Thanks for your effort and expertise. Best wishes.
Halfway through the project, the client calls to ask whether you need payment for services to date.	I thank you.
"Our firm has been operating for a year, but we will give you a founder's share if you will join."	We respect you and your abilities.
The boss tells you, "I can't give you a raise because the firm does not make enough money to afford it at this point. This is what we have to do, though, to improve income and get every-one a raise."	We have a future here.

....

AVOID THE MASTERS OF DISASTER

The other trait to look for in someone who approaches you about a job or a financial proposition is some sign that she can focus her energy sufficiently to fulfill her promises to you. Consider the following story.

Lynne wanted to sell her Honda Accord for $8,900. One woman saw the car, claimed that she absolutely had to have it, and told Lynne she would pay full price. She wanted to bring a friend by that afternoon, however, to look over the engine. This was fine with Lynne.

The woman returned with the friend, but not until the following morning. The friend looked under the hood for perhaps three minutes and concluded that the engine was in great shape. The two of them then spent twenty minutes talking about whether the woman would be happy without a leather interior. After deciding that she would only be a little disappointed with the cloth seats, the woman told Lynne that she had to get the $8,900 from her mother, who was houseboating in the lakes region but usually had her cellular phone on in the evening.

That afternoon a man phoned Lynne to ask about the car. He spent a long time asking questions about its service record. When he showed up to see it, he inspected it carefully. He then pulled a cashier's check for $8,000 out of his jacket and told Lynne he wanted to buy the car. A few minutes later he drove the Honda away and Lynne drove the check to the bank.

Letting the cash-from-cell-phone-Mom opportunity float past was a pretty easy call for Lynne. True, the woman seemed willing to pay full price for the car, but at every turn her actions said, "I don't really know what I'm doing." She did not show up on the day she said she would. Judging from how quickly her interest in the engine evaporated at the mention of the leather interior, she did not know her own mind very well. Who knows how many planets needed to be aligned before she would actually have possessed the funds to buy the car.

A lot of people in the marketplace are giving you and your partner this signal that they lack the competence to complete your dealings smoothly, if at all. Investing, negotiating, and working with me, their actions indicate, will feature a mix of wild rides and costly surprises.

Unfortunately, as many of us have discovered, not all of these folks stand out as conspicuously as Mrs. Houseboat's daughter. How do you and your partner spot these masters of disaster in advance?

When someone seems willing to agree to the payment, investment, or salary terms you want, the natural impulse is to think that she will be a good person with whom to deal. Always look closely, however, for an economy of motion. Note how this person acts around money issues. Note what she says. Pay attention to her state of mind. Consider whether her ideas seem sound to you. Respect your instincts here.

If you catch a glimpse of odd behavior, hear a curious remark, or otherwise pick up some energy that does not fit the circumstances, beware. This gratuitous gesture is often a preview of coming distractions. For example:

• A financial vice president wants to retain you plus people from two competing firms to produce his company's annual report. This strikes you as foolhardy, yet you agree. The work turns out to be just as contentious as you anticipated and eats up far more time than you budgeted. The finished product lacks punch and consistent style, and of course the vp is unhappy. You are paid, but you wish you had followed your instincts when you saw there would be too many cooks working on the broth.

• You meet the managing partner at the company that has just hired you, and his only comment to you is "Welcome to the zoo." In subsequent weeks you discover that he is routinely arbitrary and abrasive to deal with; as two other employees look on, he ends your first meeting by flipping a stack of papers in your direction and then walking wordlessly out of the room. You don't know whether to be angry with him, depressed about having taken this job, or upset with yourself for not having guessed his state of mind.

• A couple offers you full price on your home, and you sign the contract. Before escrow is even opened, they rush over with a bottle of expensive champagne, wanting to celebrate as if you were suddenly the best of friends. A week later they show up at the front door with an eleven-page single-spaced letter justifying their demand that you lower your price by $36,000. You wish you did not have friends like these.

Some people expend energy in too many different directions at once to be effective in life. They try to please too many people while attempting to run a company. They attempt to intimidate people while trying to work with them. They try to be friends when they should be thinking about whether they really want to own a house.

These folks may be misguided, undecided, or disorganized. They may be jerks. Whatever the case, their unfocused energy tells you that they lack a clear picture in their minds of how to move smoothly and directly through their dealings with you.

If you decide to deal with them, the results are predictable. These folks excel at creating problems that will distract you from your work. They sparkle at architecting negotiations that drag on, wear you out, then fall apart. When it comes to putting together investments that collapse, nobody does it better. With breathtaking speed, they absorb enormous chunks of your time, energy, and money. Dealing with these people is the pits.

Guidelines for Avoiding Masters of Disaster

What do you and your partner do when you encounter one of these masters of disaster? Stay away, attractive profits notwithstanding. If you are not yet involved with them, don't start. If you are already working with them, make plans to leave sooner rather than later. Don't let friendship, money, or blood stand in your way.

We tend to tolerate a lot of odd behavior around money. When people are demanding, steely, dead serious, scattered, shifty, or relentlessly comical about money issues, we often overlook it. We can discount straightforwardness and sincerity too quickly. The course of true business never did run smooth, the thinking goes. Money is involved, so we need to make allowances.

Nonsense.

There are plenty of people out there who are direct and on time and have the ability to think ahead. Their offers are easily understandable. They can explain the work they want you to do. They can do the work you explain to them. They can communicate new ideas to you easily. They have new ideas. They enlighten instead of confuse.

These people don't have unpredictable bouts of adolescent behavior with which you will have to cope. They don't leak energy into murky political agendas. They just want to connect, be reasonable, and complete tasks as smoothly as they can. Where possible, they hope to do some extra good, and then move along with their lives. Keep looking for one of these folks to deal with.

You may stun the masters of disaster when you turn them down. They may challenge your intelligence or competence in startlingly nasty terms. They may become toweringly indignant. Don't be sucked in. These reactions only validate your hunch about them.

Deal with people who exhibit an economy of motion, even if it seems initially as though you must sacrifice some profit to do so. As Lynne the Honda owner will attest, you can move through life more smoothly—and move on to bigger things more quickly—by transacting with these people than by tangling with those who promise you the moon but can't get their spaceships off the ground.

···

AVOID THE MASTERS OF DISASTER

The Maestros of Mayhem

···

Routine Transmission	Translation
You receive an offer to buy your house that includes a two-page addendum of extra demands and conditions.	This will be a difficult deal and a difficult experience.
A prospective employee goes on at length at how he likes working in a crazed environment.	I'm not always sure where I'm going, but I'm good at going there full tilt.
"The check should come out of purchasing next week, and then we need to process it through the check run."	We haven't the slightest clue when you'll be paid. Dealing with us will be impersonal, complex, and tiresome.
A client insists on talking to you about your services after you've gone home for the night or on your day off.	Your life is not important to me. I am not opposed to annoying you.
A prospect spends a lot of time telling you how well he knows your business.	I do not have the sense to let you, the expert, do your work.

•••

People You Can Deal With

•••

Routine Transmission	Translation
"Our credit isn't great, but I am trying to have the credit report modified by the twenty-first. Meanwhile, here is our offer."	This deal may fall apart, but it will be a straightforward experience.
The owner of a fledgling business explains his plans, then tells you, "I would be thrilled to have you as an investor, but I understand the timing may be wrong for you, or that this may not be your cup of tea."	I value our rapport, so do not feel pressured here.
"We would like to meet this afternoon, but we recognize that you have a life."	We are reasonable people.

•••

CHECK YOUR OWN FORM

One last point about messages between you and the people you deal with in the marketplace: remember to look in the mirror from time to time. Make sure that you can part with your funds gracefully and that you are not acting like a master of disaster. By being aware of your own behavior with money, you and your partner can make sure that you are not sending people

"I'm-a-tough-case" or "I'm-a-space-case" signals in error and thus causing yourselves undue fiscal frustration.

The year after my experience with the orthopedic surgeon, I witnessed an excellent example of monetary self-awareness at work. A woman drove to the real estate clinic to sign up for service. The retainer was $750. As she neared the office she realized she had left her checkbook at home. Making a return trip would really have messed up her afternoon: it would have taken almost an hour, and she needed to pick up her son from school and keep several other appointments. Yet owing to the circumstances of her case, she really needed certain work done that day.

She went to an automated teller near the office and used her credit card to pull out thirty-eight twenties, which she put on my desk as she told me this story. She could have decided to tell me her story and to ask for permission to drop off a check later in the week, but as she said, "I want you to know that I am serious."

Message received and appreciated. I didn't have change for the last twenty, and didn't really want cash anyway, but I certainly believed that she was serious about hiring me. I told her to send me a check, and I began work that afternoon. Her check arrived in the next day's mail.

Do you pay the accountant, the yard man, or the dentist promptly and with thanks? If you cannot pay a bill on time, do you call to say so and estimate when you will be able to pay it? When you buy a home, a car, or a suit, are you straightforward or fussy to deal with?

Have you ever noticed how paying up front brings an ease and a loyalty into your experience with counselors, day-care providers, and consultants you hire at work? Have you bought anyone lunch lately?

Tune in to the money messages you are sending. Appraise your actions objectively. Take time to consider what you are communicating the next time you negotiate with, invest in, or pay someone.

Wasting time and effort is neither compelling nor satisfying. Remember that the point is not to become malleable or gullible or nice in some self-destructive way. The point is for you and your partner to think about what you want to accomplish in your dealings with others and to use your funds to stride powerfully in that direction.

••

Check Your Own Form

••

Routine Transmission	**Translation**
You tell your accountant, pool person, or mechanic that you want to pay her under an odd arrangement, or you complain about her fees even though you say you want to work with her.	I want your work, but I don't want to pay you. Taking me on as a client will be painful.
You change to a bank that offers same-day credit for deposited checks so that your vendors and employees can be paid more swiftly.	Your people matter to me.
Your offer to buy a house includes the proposal to put a 10 percent deposit into escrow immediately upon acceptance.	Even though I will get these funds back if the deal does not close, I want you to know I am serious about the deal.

••

MESSAGES FROM YOU TO YOU

The third set of money messages requiring your attention is the set you send to yourself. Consider these personal telegrams.

Katherine shops at secondhand stores and garage sales almost every weekend. The clothes she brings home rarely fit well. The furniture all looks as if it came from a garage sale.

She hardly ever goes to the grocery story without a wad of coupons in her purse. Books cost too much, she claims, so she no longer buys them. To save on the electric bill she turns off the lights in the house at 8:00 A.M. even if her husband is reading the newspaper. Years ago she considered returning to teaching but decided against it, figuring that after taxes, wardrobe expenses, and commuting costs, her income would not amount to much.

Why does Katherine's life seem so small and depressing? Because she has jammed it wall to wall with actions that say, "Katherine, you are not worth very much." She tells herself that she is saving money for a rainy day, but the truth is, she does not value herself.

The real irony of this story, though, is that you don't have to be poor to develop this syndrome of personal deprivation: Katherine herself has a net worth that exceeds a million dollars.

TREAT YOURSELF LIKE A THOROUGHBRED

It's easy to assume that you are living more richly than Katherine, yet how do you know for sure? You need to look beyond your net worth and what you do with your money. Taking an annual Hawaiian vacation does not prove anything. Neither does buying lots of books or avoiding garage sales.

You need to check the messages your actions with money convey to you. If you are really using money to flourish as a human being, you are using it to nourish the promise within you. This means that, as you observe your money behavior, you will notice yourself routinely taking actions that remind you. "I am a genuine thoroughbred, and my talents, spirit, and vision need nurturing."

A life without this nourishing message is surprisingly easy to slip into. The course that could take my teaching skills to the next level? Too expensive. The blazer I would really need for that interview as the book review expert on the local television news show? Not in the budget. The shoes that would really help my feet and back feel better? Only rich or vain people pay that much for shoes. The really fresh produce? Gee, the supermarket is so much cheaper. Work on my watercolors? It will be years before I can earn any income from that.

When you act like this, you live a miserly existence by default. You fail to take actions—the teaching course, the good shoes, the painting practice—that would make your life bigger and more interesting. Like Katherine, you live exclusively for the bucks.

A miserly existence creates a miserable state of mind because you start to believe that you are not very valuable. Not spending the money to take care of your feet, for example, leads to "I have bad feet." Not working on your teaching becomes "I can't really teach that well." Without the fresh produce, you can't prepare a meal for your relatives that matches your affection for them, and you begin to think, "Nothing I do turns out right."

If ignored, the inaction and the negative waves combine to create a debilitating spiral. You starve your self-esteem. You think small. You fail to develop your talents and miss out on the income they could generate. Instead of flourishing, you steer yourself toward being unaccomplished, unhappy, unfit, and no fun to be with.

You are a magnificent, talented human being, a genuine thoroughbred. Your talents, spirit, and vision need nurturing. By focusing on your money messages, you can release yourself from the numerical prisons so easily constructed with money and make sure that you are taking actions that will open your life up, not shut it down and hollow it out.

To stay out of the miserly-and-miserable spiral, develop a sensitivity to what you say to yourself with your money behavior, then adjust your conduct to communicate the nourishing message you intend to convey. As you do this, be resourceful in preserving and developing your most precious resource—you.

Look at where and when you spend your money and what you say to yourself with these actions. Look at where and how you work. Do these activities make you happy? Do they leave you with a feeling of well-being?

Listen to yourself as you talk about money and your work. Do you take your talents seriously? Are you supporting your soul or are you merely adept at keeping the refrigerator stocked? Where are you nourishing yourself with money? There are plenty of good ways to accomplish the task.

If that shirt makes you feel ugly, ship it off to charity, even if you bought it only last month. Order two bowls of fresh strawberries for dessert. Buy yourself a new tablecloth to replace the one you've used at picnics for the past twenty-five years. Replace the oldest piece of clothing you own.

If you dislike your employer, find a new one. If you dislike your job, find work that fits you, even if it entails an initial drop in income. Tell your partner that your work is worth his full support and that you expect it. If your brother has a habit of criticizing your plans for producing a comic strip, tell him to stop it. If he continues, avoid him until he begins behaving.

Instead of hurrying across town when you are late for a meeting, taxi. If your house is full of bad memories and you need to sell it so you can move on, don't be tight about the price. Sell the house. Instead of scouring three stores for the best buy on cat food, buy it at the first one and move on with your life.

Naturally there will be times when you have to conserve funds. At these times, many people think they need to be frugal. Don't be too quick to do this. Frugality is only miserliness with a little touch-up paint, and you cannot afford to stop using money to transmit nourishing signals to yourself. When cash is scarce, it's more important than ever to remind yourself how valuable you are.

••

TREAT YOURSELF LIKE A THOROUGHBRED

A Miserly Existence

••

Routine Transmission	Message Received
Not wanting to pay $100 for shoes, you regularly buy $50 pairs, even though they provide poor support, wear out quickly, and look cheap.	I'm not worth the investment.
Although your job bores you, you continue to trudge in there day in and day out.	I don't have the talent to do anything else.

Feeling wasted in your job, you spend $3,500 on a Hawaiian vacation.	Although finding work that fits me would be great, my talents are not worth saving for, so I'll just zone out for a while.
You know you want to write screenplays full-time, but you are afraid to mortgage the house, tap your savings, or apply for a grant to raise the money to support yourself.	I couldn't pull it off, so I'll just sit on the sidelines.
You start investigating how you could become a computer engineer because it is listed as one of the hottest and best-paying jobs in America.	Will work for money.
You start thinking about moving to Dallas because you understand that real estate prices there are set to soar.	Will move for money.
Many of your financial decisions are tax-driven.	I'm not calling the shots in my life. The IRS is.
Although you shop at Price Costco and other discount clubs, they annoy you because you typically come home with huge quantities of products that are not exactly what you want. Still, you go.	It's not what I want, but the savings are unbeatable.
Your husband, who can afford it, wants to buy you a new Jaguar, but you are not sure you deserve one.	I am not worthy.

•••

A Resourceful Way of Life

•••

Routine Transmission	**Message Received**
Realizing that the $11 sun-screen feels much better and seems to work better than the $3.95 substitute, you swear off the $3.95 brand.	My health and comfort are worth the expense.
Tired of feeling like you scrape pennies off the street, you stop clipping coupons.	My time and effort are worth more than this.
Determined to free up some time to sculpt, you buy a washer and dryer so you no longer need to go to the coin laundry.	My talent is worth developing.
One of your least favorite clients picks up a cigarette butt and tricks you into taking it. You subsequently end your relationship with that client.	I can earn a living without this burr in my saddle.
You arrange for two weeks off, one for hiking in the Grand Canyon, the other for figuring out a new direction for your work.	I want more from life, and I'll get it.
You tell your partner it's not a question of whether you should work but of how you will work.	I have promise.

You apply to the Ford Foundation for a grant to make a documentary film, and you take $3,000 out of your IRA to buy a camera and equipment.	I can do this, and I will.
Your friend keeps referring to your "little firm" or your "little novel." This annoys you, so you see him less often.	People who say it can't be done should not bother those who are doing it.

•••

TRANSACTIONS SPEAK LOUDER THAN WORDS: BE AWARE

When Jake started his physical therapy practice, he and Ellen cut back on vacations, put off having the house painted, and got by with a twelve-year-old Toyota and a seventeen-year-old Saab. They made a conscious decision, however, not to resign themselves to a life of misery. They still paid for a sitter every Friday night so they could have a date. They still paid the monthly fee to belong to the pool so they could work out. They kept investing money in Ellen's designing and Jake's practice.

These actions, along with the dollar bills on Ellen's purse, kept nourishing messages flowing through the house. These actions also helped them establish Jake's practice, land Ellen some good assignments from local electronics firms, improve their cash flow dramatically, and make these transitions in a way that strengthened the bond between them.

Jake and Ellen know that they have promise as human beings, and they have committed themselves to fulfilling it. By tuning in to their money messages, they keep themselves engaged in actions that help them grow and grow together.

You too must cultivate an awareness of your money messages. Bringing forth your promise is the most important transaction of your life. Make sure you are using your dollars in a way that helps you make the deal.

Don't be discouraged, however, if at first you have trouble interpreting the signals you are sending or receiving. While you practice your messages, there's a relatively simple way to avoid many of the major problems money can cause. Just rely heavily on money's third fundamental, the simplest one of all to employ.

PRACTICE

1. Name some messages related to ownership of money and support for work that have flowed recently between you and your partner. Are you satisfied that these are the signals you want to be sending and receiving? How can you improve these signals?

2. Identify some money messages about dealing with tightwads and masters of disaster that you have recently received either at work or in a negotiation. Did you pick up these messages in time to use them?

3. Make a list of seven money messages you have sent yourself in the past two weeks. Are you nurturing yourself? Keep in mind that the amount spent does not determine the amount nurtured. How could you treat yourself better?

4. Make a Goodwill trip. Take any garment that no longer fits or that you haven't worn for a year. Throw away anything that is clearly worn out.

5. Buy yourself fresh running shoes, a yoga class, swim goggles that don't leak, a club membership extension, or something else that will put zip into your athletic life.

6. Take the person who supports your life the most to a simple thank-you lunch.

7. Name five people you really enjoy talking to about your life. Name five people you encounter regularly whom you do not enjoy talking to about your life. Invent three ways to reallocate your time to run into those in the first group more often.

Circuit Training

Take a few minutes to describe what your life would look like if things really started going your way. Now start over and describe how it would look if life became truly incredible. Begin once more, and write down how life would look if it became off-the-charts splendid.

4 The Profit in Being Deliberate

When I lived in San Francisco, one of my favorite runs was to go along the Bay all the way to the foot of the Golden Gate Bridge, then turn and head home. The bridge dominates the first half of this run. It is so incredibly massive. It is majestic. It is so orange. Running toward the bridge, you find it virtually impossible to focus on anything else.

No matter what problems I was wrestling with or what high I was riding, the bridge run always shifted my perspective. As I loped back toward the city, the problems never seemed quite as insurmountable as they had earlier. They could be overcome. And the good times seemed like something to build on, not something to stop at, rest on, and admire. Good news or bad, the run almost always brought a sense of proportion and rhythm back into my day.

A sense of rhythm is critical to using money to fulfill your promise. You and your partner look within yourselves to gain a sense for the life you can create, and then you work together on creating it in the world at large. You can find this beat and capitalize on it, though, only if you resist all the financial invitations to hurry up. To speed up your evolution, you need to slow down.

Being deliberate is money's third fundamental. When you

and your partner move your bodies and your minds too fast with money, you tend to cost yourselves cash and lose your intellectual poise. You also tend to scorch your relationship, and you work way too hard.

Moving deliberately with money helps you put yourself in sync with your partner, put cash in the bank, and maintain your peace of mind. It also enables you to set yourself up to do work with very appealing horizons.

Note that the message here is not that it would be nice if we could slow down; we'd have to forgo some possessions, promotions, or income, but we'd have a nicer balance in our lives. The message here is that you will thrive in all respects if you ease the pace at which you earn, spend, invest, negotiate, and communicate about money. You won't have to forgo anything of import, you will find it easier to stay in sync with each other, you will have plenty of bankable financial success, and you will lead a more nourishing life. All of this just for taking your foot off the financial accelerator.

At first glance the idea of making progress by slowing down may seem out of touch. After all, the world of personal finance is clearly laced with speed: the sale ends Saturday; the market is taking off; these entrepreneurs became millionaires in just fourteen months; retire sooner and live better. All around us speed seems required, if not revered.

In fact, however, speed is the optical illusion in our experience with money. It is often what people talk about, and it is often how they move, but it is not how to obtain the results you want.

You and your partner will keep yourselves on track to fulfill your promise by employing a deliberate tempo in the following four ways.

SHIFT FROM SPRINT TO SAMBA

Tammy and Bob had been looking at houses on and off for about eighteen months. One Sunday they saw one they really liked, and decided to buy it even though they had signed a one-year apartment lease less than a month before. They negotiated a purchase agreement and opened escrow.

Bob then abruptly left town on business and was gone for most of the six-week escrow period. While on the road, he directed Tammy in waging a small war with their landlord over the one-year lease, ultimately agreeing to forfeit two months' rent to terminate it.

Three days before the scheduled closing date, Bob decided he did not want to buy the property. He then began to battle with the seller in an effort to get his $8,000 deposit back. At one point, even though the contract gave him the right to keep the deposit as compensation for such a late default, the seller offered to refund $4,000. Tammy wanted to take the refund and put the episode behind them, but Bob sensed an opening and battled on, sure he could do better. The seller subsequently withdrew his offer, and the default cost the couple the entire eight grand.

With no apartment lease and no home to move into, the couple moved in with Tammy's parents. For a time they continued to look at houses to buy. The postscript to the story is that within a year they filed for divorce.

What did this couple want from their landlord? What did they want from the seller? What did they want from each other? Bob and Tammy's haste kept them from fully understanding what they were doing and why. It put them out of step with themselves, with each other, and with the world around them.

Instead of using their money to make their life together happen, they used it to create problems that consumed them.

Do you and your partner frequently feel upset about how your finances are going? Does it seem as if your financial aims always remain far away? Do you spend what seems like a lot of time planning and executing finances? Does life seem a bit hollow?

If any of these feelings seem uncomfortably familiar, consider a basic solution: slow down. Stop racing physically and mentally from one financial engagement to the next.

To create a marriage of true minds for yourselves, the two of you need to be in sync physically, intellectually, and spiritually. You cannot accomplish this complete a union when you move too fast with money.

Selling a house, buying a couch, negotiating with an investor, paying your taxes, doing your job—you'll need to weigh significant consequences in the course of performing each of these tasks. You'll have meetings to arrange, disclosures to sign, and small armadas of paper to organize. There will be phone calls to make, instructions to read, and parking spaces to find.

Sometimes when you try to sprint through all these events too quickly, you feel unhappy, alienated, and pushed to the limit.

Other times moving fast means riding the thrill of the deal, the transaction, the lawsuit, the buy, or the sale. This can feel like a heady experience, yet it still carries dangerous side effects.

In both cases finance devours your attention and eats up your time. Your rapport can erode quite quickly when you are unavailable for coupling. If you starve your rapport enough, like Bob and Tammy, you run the risk of burning it out.

The internal injuries caused by high-speed finance are painful ones. Fortunately, the steps for preventing them are easy to take.

Guidelines for Staying in Sync

To use your money to flourish as a couple, you must learn to recognize the hurry-up signals all around you, understand that your reaction to each one is a choice, and then choose to move deliberately.

Your real estate agent may call at 9:30 P.M. with a counteroffer. Ask her to call back tomorrow. The Sunday paper may run a feature on a financial planner who says, "If you don't start contributing to an IRA today, you will regret it." Give yourself the gift of ignoring the article. You may want to go purchase that patio furniture set right after dinner. Sleep on the idea instead.

The point is not that you and your partner must abstain from dealing, saving, or shopping. It's simply that you don't need to handle money matters in a hurry. When you develop the habit of responding to these signals by maintaining a deliberate tempo, you keep the stress level around the house to a minimum and improve your chances of being in step.

Enjoyably enough, one very good way to help yourselves shift gears from flat-out sprint to samba is to spend time with each other. Set up a weekly date and don't break it for anything short of a bona fide emergency. Indulge yourselves in simple luxuries—a couple of strawberry smoothies, a trip to a classic movie theater, an afternoon at a modern art museum, or a meal at a moderately priced restaurant. Go to the beach. Go for a bike ride. Treat yourselves well.

Taking care of yourselves will put you in a nurturing frame of mind. It will set a nurturing pace. It will give you time to listen to each other. It will help you remain in sync with each other and with yourselves.

••

A Sampling of Invitations to Sprint

••

The Invitation	The RSVP
"You're looking at one of the best bargains under the sun."	You buy a patio set.
"The semiannual savathon ends tonight."	You stock up on fashion.
"I want it."	You buy it.
A colleague at work tells you a story about a forty-year-old father with no life insurance who died of a heart attack over the weekend.	You call State Farm.
You fill out worksheets that help you calculate the cost of college tuition in sixteen years or the cost of retirement in twenty-four.	You leap into the stock market and begin angling for a higher-paying job.
"Not once in the past fifteen years has the U.S. stock market been the world's top performer."	You invest in foreign markets.

"Experts say the failure to build a nest egg will come to haunt the baby boomers."	You never go out to dinner.
"Interest rates are going up."	You make an offer on the next house you see.

••

STRATEGIES FOR IMPROVING YOUR SAMBA

1. Weigh overnight any transaction involving $500 or more before proceeding.

2. Do not negotiate the sale of your partner's grandmother's house on your own when in fact neither you nor your partner has expertise in real estate negotiations or contracts.

3. Keep a list near your calendar of relatives and friends you buy birthday and holiday gifts for each year; jot down ideas as they come to you during the year.

4. If you know your partner feels that you two lack the funds to buy a new car, don't spend the afternoon pricing new Hondas.

5. Stay out of the mall for a month.

6. Cancel subscriptions to all newspapers but one.

7. Make time for working out.

8. Do not have days in which the two of you look at new apartments all morning, have a soda for lunch, and shop for housewares all afternoon. Conduct the two shopping events on different days, and eat a healthy lunch.

9. Roll on the floor with some children.

10. Throw out any chart showing the stock market's performance since 1926.

Your initial reaction to this life-isn't-a-high-speed-chase advice may be to think that it will do wonders for your relationship but be brutal on your bankbook. In the world of money, where some experts say there are only two types of people, the quick and the dead, taking your time sounds like suicide. Better to move with the speed of a professional if you hope to come out ahead, right?

Pleasantly enough, that's not how it works at all.

LOPE AND BE RICH

Years ago a company hired me to help them terminate some leases on office spaces they had rented around the country. One negotiation in the Midwest was unusual for two reasons. The seven partners who owned the building were about as reliable as the Marx Brothers. Among other things, all seven referred to the building as "premium office space" even though, upon inspection, anyone could see that the property was a converted muffler shop. In addition, the cost of the buyout was steep—$250,000.

I suggested to the vice president running the project that we hire a local attorney or escrow company to exchange the buyout check for the signed termination agreement. No need, the vp assured me. For a quarter of a million bucks? It would be a waste of time and several hundred dollars, he contended. Just send the check and have them mail the document. I made a note that I had been told to do this, and then did it.

A week passed. No document. I called the lead partner. He said they had some concerns about how the agreement was written. Naturally I asked the $250,000 question: "Where's the check?"

"We cashed it," he replied. He then went on to explain that the entire team had also driven down to the bank the day after cashing it and attempted to persuade the manager to remove the funds from their account and give them back the check, but that apparently banks couldn't put the proverbial egg back in the shell once the omelette was under way.

After a couple of weeks of sending more documents, cajoling the team, and waiting, the transaction was properly documented. The client's only loss was the interest on the $250,000. From the vp's perspective, however, it was not a profitable month. Neither his boss nor the client saw the comedy in seven guys stuffing themselves into a used Saab, rolling down to their bank, and parading into the lobby intent on uncashing a check. People in the office speculated freely about whether the team would somehow try to take off with the funds. This only seared the gaffe more indelibly into everyone's mind. I'm sure none of this helped the vp make his case for a promotion and a raise at his next performance review.

By coincidence, in the same month I represented a client buying land from a developer. During a long phone call the developer and I covered all the contract issues save one— the price. We were $100,000 apart. His next words were "The price your client proposes will leave us well short of our projections. That makes it very tough on us." The line then went silent.

My impulse, naturally enough, was to say something in reaction to the silence. For whatever reason, that day I hesitated the smallest bit and, in doing so, realized I didn't have to speak. This was a revelation. I sensed that if I said, "It's still a good deal for you" or "My client can pay all cash" or even "Um," he would take it as an invitation to joust, we would go back and forth over the hundred grand, and my client would have to give up some or all of that sum. The developer had not asked a question. He had not proposed a compromise. There was no real reason for me to say anything. All this zipped through my brain in a couple of instants, and I decided to remain silent.

After what seemed like days but was probably less than half a minute, the next words I heard were, "But...I guess it's good for us [his company] to just get the deal done, so we'll do it." The significance of this exchange was immediately apparent to me: I had saved a client $100,000 simply by immobilizing my jaw.

It's virtually a law of physical science, like the pull of gravity or the atomic configuration of oxygen: speed costs you dollar bills. Whether you are buying, selling, investing, or negotiating, whether the amount in question is $2 or $2 million, moving too fast wastes your time, leads to anxiety you could have avoided, and causes mistakes that cut into your net worth.

Speed feeds the struggle with money for two reasons. First, it puts us out of sync with the world. In the case of the shaky seven, the $250,000 check should have been used to move them into position to hand over the signed agreement. By rushing past this step, the vp complicated the negotiation, embarrassed himself, and hurt his credibility with his employer.

Physical speed also keeps intuition—sometimes yours, sometimes someone else's—from surfacing. The key to the second negotiation was that I gave myself a split second to see that I could remain silent without jeopardizing the deal, and the developer had time to see that he really wanted to do the deal. I didn't harangue him into seeing things my way or manipulate him into accepting. I just let him be with his thoughts for a moment, and my client profited handsomely.

How can you and your partner avoid the financial problems

speed causes and reap some of its rewards? Just slow down. Give the world a chance to be in sync with you, a chance to work for you. The lope-and-be-rich law does not discriminate. It can work for anyone.

Susan and Kevin inherited a large warehouse that was sitting vacant. They received an offer to lease half of it for three years. The company making the offer had struggled in the past, but its earnings were up during the past six months. The rent the firm proposed was a bit under market, but tenants were scarce at that time.

What to do? In this couple's case they went on vacation. The brokers on the deal went ballistic. They wanted to hammer out the deal immediately. Kevin thought that this was perhaps the right idea, but he and Susan had made the reservations weeks before, so they told the brokers, "See you in ten days."

In thinking about the offer during their vacation, the couple realized that it was not horrible, but it wasn't really very good, either. In one particular sense accepting it would be a real hassle: it would leave them with the task of leasing the less desirable portion of the warehouse all by itself. Upon returning, they declined the offer.

Several weeks later another offer surfaced. This one was for the entire building plus the land behind it. It was for ten years, and from a company with an ocean of cash in the bank. The total value of the first offer was $540,000. The second was worth $6.6 million. After thinking about it overnight, they accepted this offer.

Guidelines for Loping

There will always be a limitless supply of reasons why you and your wallet need to act now. Remember that you can ignore them all, yet still flourish as a human being and build a fabulous bankbook.

The market will take off. The sale will end. The offer will expire. The premium will rise. The value will drop. The value will rise. What happens if...? None of this is connected to your talents, spirit, and vision in any timeless way. These are simply circumstances. Rest assured that there will always be more circumstances as long as the planet keeps spinning.

Don't work on too many financial issues at once. When you accumulate some funds, don't let them burn a hole in your pocket. Bank them instead. Stop reading *Money* and the *Wall Street Journal.* Hit the beach.

Will moving deliberately always secure you a great deal? No. There will be times when you pay full price. Will you miss some opportunities? Yes. People with bargains, job openings, and investment deals that require instantaneous action will not wait for you. Are there times, then, when your move should be faster than deliberate? No.

When you move fast, you increase the chance that you will make a move with your mind fixed on dollars instead of your promise. This typically precipitates struggles, embarrassment, and losses you can do without.

When you move deliberately enough to keep your own best interests in mind, good things tend to happen over the long run. As Susan and Kevin will tell you, sometimes your best deals are the ones you decline.

LOPE AND BE RICH

1. Do not decide to invest in a rental condo in Hawaii during your first trip to Maui.

2. If you inherit or earn a windfall, leave the funds in the bank instead of immediately making arrangements to purchase a new house.

3. Make time for working out.

4. Throw out any chart showing the compound value of money over time.

5. Wait until you two agree on whether to buy a new house before signing an offer to buy one.

6. Next time you think you need a new suit, wait a week and see if you still think so.

7. Research the issue of where to invest your money together. If you cannot find time to collaborate on this, postpone investing until you do.

8. Don't bother to sue a difficult client in small claims court over his unpaid $1,300 bill. Instead, put the twenty to forty hours of effort into more fruitful work.

KEEP YOUR INTELLECTUAL POISE

The third way you and your partner can profit from maintaining a deliberate tempo with money is to keep your mind-speed under control.

Leaping to conclusions during an encounter with money will completely disrupt your intellectual poise. Some of these intellectual triple jumps will cause you to feel inappropriately miserable. Others will point your life toward purely financial goals that will never satisfy you, which makes for dissatisfaction both before and after the chase. Either way, these reflex reactions erode your peace of mind, without which you two are far more likely to fall out of sync or mishandle your funds.

Here are four of the most dangerous mind-sets and how you two can avoid leaping into them.

All Is Lost

When I first began running my own firm, I often worried about whether the transactions I was working on would close. I would think, what if they don't? I'll run out of money, I'll be unable to find new deals to work on, eventually Nancy and I will go broke, we won't be able to pay our bills, and so on.

Over time I made two observations. These thoughts were all downside and no upside. They were real downers to bring home to the dinner table. They had no impact on the deals whatsoever, except that they impaired my ability to devote my full attention and talent to the work at hand. If a client called to talk about how to move a deal forward when I was letting my mind run off like this, I had to shift gears fast or risk sounding depressing and eminently expendable.

The other observation was how I responded to the outcome of the deals. If they fell apart, I tended to move on without lingering. If they closed, I felt sort of embarrassed for having spent time worrying about it and bringing it home for Nancy to worry about. What a waste of time, I remember thinking. Why didn't I just keep on living my life, working on ways to develop my expertise, expand my work, and enjoy life with Nancy? Why not believe in myself a little more? The only troublesome part of the whole moneymaking process, it turned out, was completely my creation. With some self-discipline, I have cut way back on the habit of thinking that all is lost.

Not making a deal, not paying your taxes on time, having to take some money out of savings—these events can lead to scary thoughts: If I don't make this deal, it's curtains. If I don't receive that check by Thursday, it's all over. I'm twenty-six and don't own a home, so I probably never will.

These thoughts can consume you. Worrying—that is, conjuring up dire possibilities and trying to predict what will happen to you—cripples your ability to think constructively in the here and now about how to develop your talent, nurture your relationship, or even enjoy dinner.

How can you two avoid being consumed? Have an alternate source of self-esteem. For me, it is running. For Nancy, it is dance. For you, it could be gardening, windsurfing, or yoga. Any nonfinancial activity in which you can regularly lose yourself will do. This will physically disengage you from the circumstances that trigger the desperate thoughts and give you an opportunity to refresh and replenish yourself.

If indeed the deal craters, the taxes go unpaid, or the check bounces, you will have to adjust accordingly. But while such events are sometimes uncomfortable and while they will have an impact on your life—you may have to pay a 10 percent penalty or increase your income to beef up your savings again—that impact will be a fatal one only if you let it.

You are not your bankbook, job, or tax return. You are a being much richer than that. Just because your finances do not go precisely according to your current idea of what's good does not mean that life will not be great.

There is a life after a late fee. All is never lost.

Everything Will Be Perfect

I once earned $225,000 on a single commission. This is hardly a retire-to-a-villa-in-the-South-of-France sum, yet remember that even if you earn a million dollars a year, your biweekly paycheck is only about $40,000. It was a hefty check, and it was an enormous amount in my mind.

As I worked on the transaction and it became apparent that I might indeed earn this windfall, I was appropriately enthusiastic. I was also quite curious. What would it be like to earn a hunk of cash that big? How would life change?

The deal closed, the day came to pick up the check, and I drove to the bank with it. While in the car, I made sure I still had it, approximately 287 times. When I arrived at the bank, there was no brass band. As always, the teller handed me a deposit receipt and wished me a nice day. I went home and I was still Bill Devine, no more and no less. The cash was nice to have, but I still knew I did not want to be a real estate broker for the rest of my life, and I still had to tie my shoes to keep them on.

What if you pay off the mortgage, get the raise, or push your 401(k) over the $50,000 mark—or over the $500,000 mark? Will everything be perfect? This overinflated expectation is the companion reflex to the "all is lost" plunge to misery, and like the plunge, it threatens you with deep distraction.

The danger here is that you will pour yourself into the achievement of some financial aim. If you do, you will spend too much of your life in pursuit of a brass ring that cannot possibly fulfill you, even if you grasp it.

How do you keep from being swept away on this financial riptide?

Perform a little test. Think of something that, at some point in your life, you wanted desperately. Perhaps there was a suit you had to have, a necklace, a piece of furniture, or a pair of skis. Maybe you have a huge bank account or a Lamborghini, and maybe you still consider this a most prized possession.

In a moment when no one else is around, spend five minutes

with this item. Touch it. Examine it. Really try to absorb its essence.

Next, find a relatively quiet time when you can give your partner a long, long hug. Look deep into her eyes.

Finally, compare the two experiences and then take a stand. Life is too short to spend sitting on the fence. Resolve to spend more time cultivating whichever experience seemed more promising—owning a prized possession or connecting with your partner.

The Deal Is Done

I recently heard about a man who had a handshake deal on a new job from a company president. The salary was impressive and the stock options were generous. The hiring decision just needed approval from the board of directors, which the president assured his friend was merely a rubber-stamp maneuver.

Time went by. The president assured his friend that the delay was purely procedural. The executive-to-be was feeling great, so he and his wife bought a new Mercedes. The day of the board meeting finally came, and their friend called to say there would be no job, there would be no new division, and that he expected to be forced to resign.

Leaping to conclusions about the progress of a transaction is an easy way to bring heartache into your life. Perhaps you are expecting a job offer or negotiating the return of a blouse. Maybe you are in the midst of a deal to buy an airplane, or maybe you are simply awaiting your paycheck. People will tell you that the deal is done sometimes just to calm your anxieties or because they want you to stop shopping. Sometimes we say this to ourselves just because we so desperately want it to be true. If you charge ahead in life based on this belief, though, you set yourself up for major disruption.

No matter what sort of transaction you are conducting, remember that deals are done when there is nothing left to be done, never before.

We Don't Measure Up

According to the Forbes 400, Bill Gates is worth more than $18 billion. Steven Spielberg is worth about $1 billion. Even your neighbors down the street are putting an addition on their house. Just about everyone has more money than you, right?

If you leap to this conclusion, it's only a short walk to "Our life is a real eyesore."

You and your partner can use lots of financial yardsticks to compare yourselves with other people. Income, net worth, and investment results are all possible gauges.

Remember, though, that these numbers leave the richness and potential of your life together entirely unaccounted for. This is not to say that people with bigger incomes than you have less richness and potential. Their numbers don't account for the richness and potential in their lives, either. The point is that financial comparisons between human beings are meaningless.

All the comparison can do is prompt you to hurl yourselves into doing something to reach the point where you think you will compare favorably. Whenever you do this, the work of using money to create a life that reflects your unique gifts slams to a halt.

Cancel your subscription to *Forbes*. Refrain from reading the "man-look-how-much-these-guys-made" articles on the business page. Steer conversational companions away from droning on about how much money so-and-so rakes in every year.

Whatever it takes to avoid making these sideways appraisals, just do it, because comparison living will only perpetuate your struggle with money.

Guidelines for Intellectual Poise

In the course of your life together, you and your partner will surely have some pleasant moments with money as well as some difficult ones. These will give you ample opportunity to live a lunge-and-plunge lifestyle—that is, to declare yourselves to be on the brink of absolute bliss, to feel permanently mired in misery, and to veer back and forth between the two extremes, either individually or in tandem.

Savor your high points. Acknowledge your disappointments. Refrain from rushing to the conclusion that your feeling du jour is the final word, however, regardless of whether your latest money experience was a disaster or a delight. Work on developing some intellectual poise in how you react to encounters with money.

There will always be money problems, but because you and your partner have talent and imagination, you will always be capable of creating solutions. By not vaulting to hasty conclusions about your experience with money, the two of you can put problems in perspective, stay in stride, and keep focusing your efforts on building a rich life together.

RUN OVER THE GROUND, NOT INTO IT

Early in my career I worked as a salesman at a commercial real estate company. The ethic at the firm was to work really hard and make a lot of money. The management wanted brokers in motion: if you weren't negotiating or closing a deal, you were expected to get out of the office and make cold calls. I earned an unremarkable living, financially and otherwise, in that environment.

One spring I mentioned that I planned to take the exam to upgrade my license from salesperson to broker. The company's hard-work ethic flexed its muscle. Others at the firm quickly pointed out that the test was horribly difficult and that all the studying would cut into my income. Intent merely on distancing myself a bit from the pack, I signed up for the exam anyway, studied for all of four hours the night before, and passed. The interesting development, though, was that within minutes of opening the notice from the Department of Real Estate, I realized I wanted to start my own firm.

The company's hard-work ethic kicked into gear again when I announced my intention to resign. I can serve my clients better this way, I explained, but I was quickly reasoned down. The administration of the firm would be too difficult to handle along with the transactions. Making money outside a large company would be impossible. The formula for success, went the conventional wisdom, was to make the calls, do the deals, collect the commission checks, and let management manage. Work in, money out. One hundred calls will equal ten prospects will equal one deal. Employees, management, and even competitors all predicted that I would come crawling back within a year.

When I arrived at work my first day on my own, my firm consisted of a computer, a phone with voice mail, an $85-a-month office, and four clients. Four years later the rent had risen to $110, but I had the same computer, the same phone with voice mail, and the same four clients. I had also put in a lot of weeks when I worked no more than twenty-five hours, and I had made almost a million dollars.

Shifted Horizons

The first thing I noticed in my new office was the quiet. There were no orders to follow. No sales goals to chase. No standardized brokerage truths being hurled my way. When I was not on the phone, the office was entirely still.

Removed from the pressure to work hard, I was free to think. I decided that instead of trying to set myself up as the only one with the answers, I would teach my clients everything I could about the nuances of real estate deals. Entire companies of brokers attempted to lure these customers away from me during this period, all to no avail. These clients remained fiercely loyal to me, basically because I helped them become better at their jobs. This loyalty meant that I didn't have to spend time impressing a new set of contacts every month.

Not having to hustle around making dozens of cold calls a week gave me time. With this time I could take complete care of my four clients. With this time I could also take care of me. I stayed rested and in shape. I studied my work carefully and realized that I needed to move on from real estate brokerage because the work would not satisfy me in the long term.

I also took a jazz dance class in which this sexy woman in a fantastic yellow leotard was the substitute teacher one Saturday. I took the time to find out her name, to hear about how much she liked to write, to see that she was a really beautiful and talented person, and to marry her.

Had I remained locked in my old firm's hard-work routine, I doubt that I could have created the distinctive style, the confidence, the income, or the career path that I developed during those four years. I also never would have met my wife.

All I really wanted from the decision to take the exam was to distinguish myself a bit from everyone else who worked for my former employer. The dividends that decision paid amounted to a jackpot I never could have imagined. How can you and your partner put yourselves in positions to reap some of these rewards? You need to steer clear of one of the most overlooked and costly combinations of money and speed: hard work.

The basic problem with hard work is that it is an entirely synthetic objective. It is largely unrelated to whether you and your partner will flourish as human beings.

This is not to say that you don't have to apply yourself to your work. On the contrary, the point is that to create the life you are capable of, you must apply your entire self, not just the part of you that can arrive at the job on time, perform specified tasks as directed, then repeat the process day after day. You have much more promise than that.

Unfortunately, many people speed right past this distinction between hard work and applying yourself and run themselves straight into the ground. Part of the reason for the culture-wide glorification of hard work is that it has such a vast and star-studded PR department. Listen to celebrities describe their rise from obscurity. Watch professional athletes explain their game plans. Read what CEOs say they want in their employees. Hard work is very often the centerpiece of their sound bites. A lot of people come to hard work out of a sense of hero worship.

Embracing hard work is also frequently more convenient than thinking about how to develop and express your talent. When some folks aren't quite sure where they're headed or whether their efforts are helping them expand their lives, they take refuge in hard work. In an effort to feel that there is meaning in jobs they dislike, they declare that hard work is a good thing in and of itself. Well, I'm working hard, the thinking goes, so good things will happen to me eventually. They can then throw themselves into the job as if time and energy expended will accumulate and amount to something satisfying at some point in life.

Just because hard work is culturally acceptable, however, doesn't mean it's a good idea.

The problem with the rush to do the work and acquire the hard-worker label is that it lulls you into ignoring your talent, spirit, and vision. This causes frustration that affects many aspects of your life.

When you fail to work on your promise, you miss out on building your ability to conceive of new and valuable ideas and bring them into existence, either by working in concert with others or by working on your own. This denies you the income your talent could produce.

Without this practice, you have to rely on someone else to give you a job and tell you what to do. This does little for your sense of self-worth.

Coming home at 8:00 P.M., having your schedule dictated by someone else, being on edge because of the company's breakneck pace—this puts you in a frame of mind that makes you difficult to snuggle up to. This lifestyle also makes it easy for simple misunderstandings between you and your partner to flare into entrenched battles.

If you are well acquainted with some of these issues, take

heart. Sometimes all you need to do is reclaim command of the pace of your work, and you put yourself on a path to earning money in a way that will nourish your relationship, your bank-book, and your soul better than you could ever have imagined.

Guidelines for Working Deliberately

Assuming more control of your pace at work begins with a guerrilla-type effort. The idea is not to be subversive or angry. The aim is not to start your own firm. The aim is to do better work and feel better about yourself. You just need a quiet, con-certed, committed effort to become more deliberate while earn-ing a living.

There are countless ways of reasserting control over your workday. Leave your email to be handled another day. Excuse yourself from watercooler discussions about the CEO's new house, the CEO's latest sales trip, or the CEO's view of the market. Let go of thinking so much about the competition, and instead make time to consider how to become more competent.

Shuffle your daily routine. Vary your commute. Take your vacation days. Learn the habit of pleasantly angling for meet-ings to be held at a time that is convenient for you.

Consciously take more deep breaths while you sit at your desk. Go to a relaxed midweek lunch with your partner on occasion. If someone asks, "Are you working hard?" or "Are you busy down at the office?" simply reply, "I'm doing bril-liant work," and leave it at that.

Remember that your task in life is not to be told what to do, nor is it to do the same thing forever. Remember that your task in life is not to work for Microsoft or AT&T or Bridgette's Car Repair Emporium. The talent you possess is much broader than that.

Your task is to find the rhythm in converting your talent into work that people find valuable, that supports you, and that fits into your life with your partner. You have lots of options.

WORKING MORE DELIBERATELY

1. For an hour a day set your phone to go directly to voice mail without ringing.

2. Telecommute or take the train to work one day every two weeks.

3. Find a way to unload the client who understands you and your work least.

4. Dress down at work more often.

5. Take an hour to write down your strengths and weaknesses at work. Use part of the time to acknowledge how good you are at what you do.

6. If someone is too loud or addresses you in an annoying way, write him a funny letter asking him to modify his behavior.

7. If office birthday parties are stressful, invent a polite excuse for skipping the next one.

8. Make sure you are getting sufficient rest.

9. When you are offered a new job or position, think it over for a few days before deciding what to do.

10. Make an effort to talk to your partner during the day, even if just for a quick connection.

It's Not the Speed, It's the Rhythm: Be Deliberate

Slowing down—it is a power move with money.

Once you begin to act more deliberately, you tend to discover an important truth: if you and your partner are genuinely committed to using money to fulfill your promise, you need to become accomplished.

PRACTICE

1. Invite your partner to take a day off from work with you. Revisit a courting spot or spend the day getting some exercise together.

2. Arrange two consecutive weekends with no plans, or turn the phone, the radio, and the television off for a week. Leave magazines and newspapers alone as well. Read books for pleasure and listen to tapes and CDs.

3. Recall two recent transactions. Perhaps you hired someone to perform some yard work, or maybe you bought or sold a car or an investment. Did you rush into these transactions or hurry through them? How might they have been different had you been more deliberate?

4. The next time you negotiate a work assignment or transaction whose value exceeds $2,000, consciously attempt to slow yourself down. Arrive early and refreshed to appointments. Leave plenty of time to conduct matters. Ask the questions that occur to you. Let others talk and let them finish their sentences. Sleep on all decisions before finalizing them. How do these adjustments change the experience and its results?

5. Name ten expenditures you regularly make that matter to

you. Note next to each one why it is so important. Name ten items or services you purchase that do not matter. Could you do without these permanently?

6. Go a day without spending any cash or writing any checks. Go a month without visiting a mall or a department store.

Circuit Training

1. Try a different commute, and go to a different place for lunch. Spend an extra thirty minutes sprucing up your work area. Dress more simply for work.

2. Name seven things you could do for a living—if you had the resources—that people would find valuable. Which two do you find most intriguing? Take one step toward investigating those two possibilities.

5 The Fruits of
Being Accomplished

A number of years ago, at a time when I was thinking about starting the clinic and writing a book about money, I thought I had figured out a way to earn some extra income. Two brokers from another firm asked me to join them in making a proposal to handle the real estate work of a large company. Having done this sort of thing for years, I regarded it as a no-brainer.

My colleagues and I put together an elaborate proposal. My impression was that it took longer than it should have.

We made a lengthy and formal presentation to the firm's senior management. Again, my impression was that it took longer than it should have. We had to wait in the lobby twenty minutes for the vp of real estate, and then we waited another ten in the conference room for the firm's executive vice president, whom I remember as being overly impressed with his cuff links and with himself.

We were selected to handle the work. When we met with the real estate vice president for a preliminary discussion of the subleases he needed arranged, he talked at length about how fortunate we were to have the assignment and about how he wanted a very high quality effort from us. This took up three-quarters of the meeting.

I was starting to bring my frustration home to the dinner

table. I was also showing up late for dinner, because the real estate vp liked late afternoon meetings.

When we met again the following week for another strategy session, the vp spent what felt like two decades talking about the size of the sign we should have in front of the vacant buildings, what color it should be, and whose telephone number should be on it.

As I drove home from that meeting I had a thought that translated roughly into this: This is a colossal waste of my time. It is insane. I could run this company's entire real estate operation with a car phone and a pack of Post-its. Instead I am going to spend half my week going to stupid meetings like this one, all so we can do a couple of simple subleases.

The following day I met with the two other brokers, explained that this was simply not working for me, and resigned from the project.

The reality was that I no longer saw myself as a real estate consultant. I had this idea that I could write books and start a radical new firm that would help people buy and sell homes with less hassle and expense. Trying to squeeze this emerging conception of myself back into my old role was disrupting my life.

The frustration was taking up space for Nancy and me. My talents were sitting undeveloped, and I was angry a lot because, taking orders from these people, I felt like a carhop at a root beer stand. But what really grabbed my attention was that all my mental churnings were keeping me from doing my portion of the assignment efficiently, which was only going to keep me from earning income both from them and from my new ideas.

The bottom line was that I felt extremely unaccomplished. Furthermore, I realized that if I did not start doing work that really fit me and my relationship, I was going to be not just unhappy but also broke.

The fourth fundamental practice of money is being accomplished at work. Not hard work. Work that fits you and your relationship.

The intimate link between money and work is hardly new. In ancient times the word "talent" referred as it does today to inner human capabilities, yet it also was the name for an extremely valuable unit of gold or silver. The exact amount varied by culture, but in all cases a talent exceeded 58 pounds of precious metal. In those early cultures the distinction between currency and natural human qualities was merely a matter of form. The historical definitions implied that working the talents within you would yield talents you could bank or spend.

In fact the yield is even better than this. When you do work that suits your talents, you are compelling: your work connects people to you, serves them, and inspires them to value you in a way that allows you to support yourself. As you discover and develop your talents, you become more deeply conscious of who you are and what you can do, and you can bring this truer expression of yourself to your life with your partner. And when you succeed in capturing this yield, you build a sense of self-worth that is available nowhere else.

By working the talent within you, then, you can create a satisfying life and fulfill many dimensions of your promise. Work that fits you and your relationship will enable you to become accomplished as a human being.

None of this is guaranteed with just any job, however. As I discovered on my last real estate assignment, not working your talents yields quite a bit less. When you and your partner fail to do work that gives full expression to your talents, vision, and spirit, you both frustrate yourselves, forgo income, and make yourselves susceptible to the pain of being laid off. You also disrupt your relationship and leave yourselves open to the sort of lopsided relationship discussed earlier, where your partner is accomplished and you are not.

If you are not accomplished, few of your efforts to invest, negotiate, budget, or save will satisfy you, because much of the richness of life will escape you. When you fail to work your talents, life does not work.

So, is the answer to do what you love? Will that secure the crucial fit between you, your work, and your relationship? In fact, the key to working well is not that simplistic. Whether you are downsized, disenchanted, or happily earning a six-figure salary, whether you work for yourself or for someone else, the key to being accomplished and easing your struggle with money is to make sure to take these steps.

CATCH A GLIMPSE OF YOUR PROMISE

You are immensely talented. Part of your promise as a human being is that you have the ability to excel at difficult tasks and to help people in important and valuable ways. The same is true of your partner. You can argue with me on these points, but you will lose.

How do you begin to convert all this promise into work that will support and satisfy you? The first step is to come up with a vision of yourself, to become more conscious of the promise within you so you can work on articulating it.

A vision of what you can do and who you can be locks you into rewarding work. In uncertain times this vision gives you direction. It helps you realize that you have outgrown your job before you go stale. It also helps you pull yourself through setbacks. When you have a vision for yourself, you are less likely to let money's math paralyze you in a dead-end job and more likely to move toward making your talents pay off.

To capture a sense of what your promise is, ask yourself what you think you can do and what you are here for.

What Do You Think You Can Do?

The purpose of this question is to encourage you to own up to your vision of yourself. The key words in the question are "you" and "think."

This is not about what your partner, your best friend, your mother, or your boss thinks you can do. Your viewpoint is the one that counts.

The question is also not about being safe or small. It is not about repeating yourself. Flex your imagination. Give it some room to roam. This is not about what you can do that you will admit to others: it's about tapping in to those bigger, deeper visions that you harbor within yourself. Unshackle yourself, but do so in a way that is true to you. Be loose.

One day shortly before my experience with the cuff-linked executive, I went for a long, satisfying run in San Francisco with a friend. As usual we talked about many topics, including work. I was looking for a new direction, and he was wondering whether the law partnership he had just joined was a genuinely good spot for him.

We ended our run in front of a bookstore downtown, and I remember looking through the window at the display of Sue Grafton's latest novel, one from the series that started with *A Is for Alibi.* I remarked to him as I pointed to the books, "I bet I could write one of those."

"Nope," he quickly responded, "that's a one-in-a-million shot." Earning a living by writing books, in his mind, was not something one could do.

Not wanting to cap such a pleasant run with a debate, I simply changed the subject, but I didn't change my mind. Sure, writing a book would take time. Clearly it also would take some practice—I hadn't written anything longer than a three-page letter in more than a decade. And certainly my idea needed fleshing out. I recall that I had some vague sense that the book would be about how money really works, but fiction or nonfiction? Title? Length? I had no idea.

I remember thinking quite distinctly, though, Who the blazes do you have to be to write a book? Walking through a bookstore, it had always seemed to me that the full spectrum of IQs was represented in the inventory. It did not seem as if you had to be Phi Beta Kappa from Princeton to write one.

I thought that I could write a book and that people would be interested in reading it. Roughly three years after stopping in front of that B. Dalton window at the corner of Sutter and Kearny, I cashed the advance check to write the book you have in your hand.

What do you think you can do?

Expand the possibilities. Move into the realm of belief without evidence. Don't be realistic. Don't demand proof. This is not a lawsuit. This is life. Perhaps there was something you once thought you could do, but now you figure you cannot. Reach back and remember. Recapture that glimpse of your promise.

Perhaps you sense you have a gift for painting, a knack for designing software, or an intuitive connection with children.

Perhaps you think you could run a car repair shop like no one else ever has. Maybe you have an idea for an Internet product, even though you have worked at a bank for the past fifteen years.

This is work that fits you and that you would find interesting, and it is knocking at your door. It is up to you to answer the call by acknowledging it.

Don't be dissuaded by how far away your vision seems, how difficult it will be to achieve, how likely success may be, or exactly how it could happen. This is not a "how" question. It is exclusively a "what" question.

Perhaps someone squashed your ideas in the past. Perhaps you have spent years squashing your own ideas. It's time to free yourself of these impediments.

To come up with work that will fulfill you and support you, you must begin to honor your own instincts about what you think you can do.

What Are You Here For?

I read recently about a businessman who was baffled by the financial woes of his latest venture, owning a minor league hockey team. He was selling tickets at $5—less than the cost of a seat at the movies, he was quick to point out—yet the games attracted so few fans that the team could not pay its bills and ceased operations.

"I can't believe it," said the owner, who had made his fortune in the life insurance industry. "Every other business I've been in, if you offer a quality product at an affordable price, that usually is an absolute formula for success."

A quality product at an affordable price. If you think about that phrase for a moment, you find the root of the man's financial problems—his work lacks vitality. It does not spring from deep within him, and it does not connect to us in any meaningful way.

The lesson here is a simple one: your work must connect to people, and it must connect from deep within you. Otherwise you will starve.

Answering the first question—What do you think you can do?—is important. You may think you can run a minor league hockey team, drive a company to $300 million in sales, or be a great litigator. This is great. Have ambition.

As important as that first question is, though, your vision needs to extend beyond just what you think you can do. It needs dimension. It needs soul. You add this to your vision by asking, What am I here for?

This second question is important because it forces you to think about how your work helps others recognize and realize their talents. Whom do you serve and how? Are you helping people raise their families? Grow? Educate themselves? Do work that is meaningful to them?

If you are not connecting with us in some important way, you will have difficulty earning income because we won't have any incentive to become your customer. Work without customers will not satisfy you.

This question also makes you think about how your work matches the size of your spirit. Do you just do what someone else tells you, or do you perform tasks that originate somewhere inside you? Do you follow some formula you read about in a business school text, or do you have a point of view? Are you just doing something you love, or are you extending yourself beyond the bounds of what has become comfortable and known to you? Is your work acceptable to you?

The truth is that you are not here to offer quality products at affordable prices. You are not here to sell vitamins to friends or to sign up your relatives as customers for a long-distance phone company. You are not here to follow moneymaking formulas and schemes as if they were pass patterns in the playbook of life. You are capable of more than that.

If you are not expressing something important and meaningful to you, you will labor at your work because you will not really have much of an interest in it.

Be careful not to take this question as a cue to embrace a life that serves others without serving you. There's nothing wrong with working in a soup kitchen or teaching children, for example. But no matter how well these tasks serve others, they are poor paths to travel if they make you feel exploited or angry. These are not the only ways to serve others.

And do not settle for a response that essentially amounts to "I'm just here to do an honest day's work." You are not a plow horse. You are a person of talent.

The truth is, we need your best effort. Maybe you can create a chain of high-quality preschool centers, a healing arts center, or a computer software program that will help people express themselves better. We have plenty of problems for which we could use an inspired solution. Favor us with your best shot.

What are you here for? Yours is the only answer that counts. Just remember that the answer must be more than ambitious. It must be personal, and it must serve others, because you need the motivation that comes from having your vision mean something to you, and you need customers.

Guidelines for Catching a Glimpse

Talking to people in fields that intrigue you, signing up for seminars at career centers, attending job fairs, taking aptitude tests—these are all fine. Keep in mind, though, that you are on the lookout for your promise as a human being. Even if you think you have a pretty good idea of your vision for yourself, make sure to try these two triggers.

First, do nothing. Sit on your front porch. Work in your garden. Pull weeds or rake your lawn. Wash the car. Engage in some recreation that makes you feel good. Let the questions work on you. Let them open you up. Unstructured activities will quiet your mind and body and allow intuition to make itself known. It's no accident that the notion of writing a book surfaced for me at the conclusion of a long run, in those moments when my body was still humming with the rhythm of the run and my mind was well relaxed.

Second, try some specifically nonanalytical approaches. Take a creativity course. Meet with a counselor you know to possess remarkable instincts. Catching a glimpse of your promise is not a mathematical exercise. Intuition and gut feel count for more than logic and precedent.

HOW SHOULD THE INCOME POTENTIAL OF WORK FIGURE INTO MY THINKING? Do not include financial potential as a criterion in coming up with your vision of yourself. Don't be drawn by an apparent bonanza, and don't be repelled by an apparent dearth of money. At this point, thinking in terms of dollars will only muddle the development of your vision and mess up the process of building your work.

Note that I am not saying you should forget about being paid. As we saw in Chapter 3, being paid is how you know your work is important to people. As we'll see in the next section, it is your responsibility to give people the opportunity to pay you. Being paid is indispensable. For now, simply make sure not to collapse the process of building your work. At this point, vision is the thing.

Focus on service instead of income. If, in your view, the work you are considering would really serve people, there will be plenty of cash available to you in ways we will address presently. If, in your view, the work does not serve people, there will be little cash possible because you will have a difficult time being compelling.

WHAT IF I NEED INCOME IMMEDIATELY? As you look for your vision, you may have to earn some income in another pursuit if you don't have savings, an investor, or a loan to cover expenses. If this is the case, pick the best course you can and have faith in your ability to make adjustments later on. Be clear with yourself, however, that this is an interim move. Stick with the questions. What can you do? What are you here for? Not having an answer can be frustrating, but don't abandon your search for a glimpse of your promise. Do the work you can, and don't pummel yourself about it. Have faith that your moment will come.

HOW WILL I RECOGNIZE WORK THAT FITS ME? Later on, you'll feel hooked on doing the work and testy when you find yourself doing things that don't contribute to you getting back to the spot—physical and intellectual—where you do that work. You will smile. You will be in good humor. People will want your work, and they will want to pay you for it. When you really have it, doing work other than work that fits you makes you a little crazy. When you think, talk, or do it, by contrast, time flies.

At the outset, however, there is just a glimpse. You let your imagination run and it feels good. Time flies, and it stops. A sense of peace, and a quiet voice inside you saying, "This fits." It's not a huge signal, but it's there.

To know more precisely about the exact terms of the promise you will make to us, you must begin to cultivate your talents.

CATCH A GLIMPSE OF YOUR PROMISE

1. Think back to when you were in grade school. What did you want to do?

2. Take a creativity class. What skills do you seem drawn to?

3. Ask an expert what your handwriting suggests about your talents and how you are capitalizing on them.

4. Discuss your promise with a counselor you know to be unusually intuitive.

5. Remember that just because you said once that you love a certain job does not mean you cannot revisit the question of what you are here for.

6. Think back to high school. What did you want to do then?

7. Have you outgrown the vision of yourself you have been working on?

CULTIVATE YOUR TALENTS

Robin's career as an artist has taken her down some unexpected paths. She has had her work printed on T-shirts and sold at street fairs. She has worked as a stylist for a photographer. She has taught art in junior high school and offered private art classes for both children and adults. She recently applied for and won a fellowship. For many years her income has been a patchwork proposition, but these efforts have enabled her to continue to paint and to show and sell her more formal work.

Amy also saw herself as a painter at one time. When she tried to earn an income with her artwork, however, she tired of the effort. After discussing the matter with her husband and several others, she decided that the prudent thing to do was to land a job with a regular salary. She became an accountant, telling herself that she would go back to her art later in life. Today she earns close to $50,000 annually, and two of the pieces she painted almost twenty years ago hang in the hallway of the office she works in.

Has either of these artists made meaningful strides from promise to fulfillment?

In fact, Robin is quite accomplished. To articulate your promise in the world and reach a significant level of accomplishment and income, you need to follow her lead.

Many people will tell you, as one successful entrepreneur once told me, that the key to becoming accomplished is wrapped up in the advice, "Don't just try—do it." In fact, this is not what Robin is doing at all. Exhortations from the keep-at-it school of achievement are not particularly helpful road maps and can actually undermine your efforts to flourish. If you want to turn the talents you possess into talents you can bank, you need to follow a more highly refined strategy.

You may think you should assist your employer in expanding her car repair shop to three locations. You may want to run your own design firm. You have a vision for yourself. You want to turn it into a life that supports you and your partner.

Whether you think your work lies in computer chips or the arts, whether you sense you'd do well in academia, in your back den, or in marketing at Microsoft, you need to understand the three elements of cultivating your talents.

Lean on Your Talents

Converting your vision into a livelihood requires that you condition the talents within you. You do this work on yourself by consciously and repeatedly choosing to put yourself in position to rely on your talents. Lean on them. Let them work for you. Making these choices is the vocational equivalent of weight training. It's how you put muscle and definition on your frame.

At every juncture, ask yourself what's the next step in moving toward your vision, and then simply take it. You are a work in progress, and you need to forge competence.

BEGIN. Robin's first step was a wise one: she began painting for a living. She bought the supplies, set up her studio, and started working on her pieces. She acknowledged her vision of herself and put herself in a position to refine her skills and abilities.

Inertia or anxiety notwithstanding, you need to begin realizing your vision, too. If you want to teach, send for an application to complete your teaching credentials. If you want to be a concert pianist, obtain a piano, make room for it, and clear time for playing it. If you want to acquire a clothing company, set up a meeting with a lawyer or an investment banker. If you are starting your own firm, arrange for a phone, office space, and business cards. If more responsibility at the firm you work for is the first step on your path, show up tomorrow focused on doing your work better.

You may never have done this before. That's okay. In fact, that's the point.

PRACTICE. Since she began painting, Robin has done well at repeatedly putting herself in a position to expand and refine her skills. She has taken advanced technique classes and logged hours in her studio. She has taught her craft. She has arranged several showings at a local gallery, and pursued the fellowship that allowed her to work with other serious artists. In a word, she has practiced.

You, too, need to practice leaning on your talents. At some

points in your career, this will mean that you'll have to study. You'll go to nursing school, for instance, or take piano lessons with an advanced teacher.

At other points it will mean you'll perform. Negotiate big deals on your own. Put together the footage for the opening scenes of your documentary. Moonlight as a pianist at a Chicago hotel. Do volunteer work at the local hospital. If you need to reverse-engineer a computer, then that's the next step, whether you've ever attempted such a task or not. If you have to straddle two jobs—studying for the bar exam and at the same time working at your old job as a real estate broker, for example—you'll straddle.

At every stage, you'll need to spend time with your talent. If you notice that you are not really relying on yourself, you will have to modify what you are doing for work. You need the practice.

"I'm learning," says a woman who works as an administrative assistant in an investment office. She can run more than fifty software programs. But what is she expressing? Unless she is expressing herself in some important way, she is wasting her opportunity.

Are you learning to do what others tell you, or are you learning to express what is valuable inside you? You need to cultivate what's inside you, not fill yourself with information. Do not waste your practice time.

STILL YOUR MIND. Everyone knows artists starve. Robin began painting anyway, and she continues. She has not let her own doubts, conventional wisdom, or other people's opinions distract her or hold her back.

You will need to still your mind as part of leaning on your talents. Refrain from making too many judgments about what can and can't be done. They will only cloud your vision. Once you have a sense of what you want to do, put your energy into doing the next step, not debating the likelihood of its success with yourself. If certain people cause you to question your talent, arrange to see those people less often.

To work your promise into reality, you need to put yourself in a position to uncover your talent and to hone it. There is great peace and satisfaction in leaning on your talent. You will find you can do more than you think you can.

There are also very tangible benefits. Leaning on your talent is how you discover what you can do for us. It's how you realize that you can compose inspiring essays, repair houses, fix broken bones, or bring a special flair to physical therapy. With the confidence that comes from practicing, you can fashion a promise you can be paid for.

Bring Your Promise All the Way to Us

Robin put us in a position to recognize her talent. She did not just sit in her studio and mourn her lack of recognition. She imagined different ways to be paid: fellowship, stylist, teacher, T-shirts, showings. Over time she has become adept at repackaging her talent and bringing it all the way to customers.

In addition to working on your talent, you must also work on the coin of the realm. You must concern yourself not just with what you are paid for but also with how you are paid. This is crucial to converting the talent within you into talents you can bank.

Each one of us is responsible for bringing our talent all the way to the customer. Just as you must cultivate your competence, so must you cultivate your talent in the sense of helping others recognize the value of your work and inspiring us to pay you for it. This is not a step you can afford to delegate to an employer. It is not a place to be unimaginative. Cultivate us and our funds. Figure out how your work relates to our promise, and take responsibility for making sure we know about it.

You can utilize all sorts of vehicles and arrangements for being paid for your expertise. You can collect a paycheck from an employer. You can write a book, make audiotapes or a video. Manufacture and sell us a product—a painting or a semiconductor. Consult by the hour. Consult by the project. Go on tour. Put your viewpoint in a comic strip. Create a radio or a television show. Write a newspaper column.

You can serve a different set of customers. You can bundle your services differently. The issue is really one of how you choose to package your talent.

Realizing that you have a choice about how you are paid is especially important when you hit a crossroads. Perhaps you have lost your job or become disenchanted with the work you do. Perhaps you want to put different skills to use. You don't have to confine yourself to being paid in the same old way.

I have read of Ph.D.'s who are out of work. They feel that they have gambled and lost. All I can do is research and teach, they say. I suspect that's not true. Their disappointment is understandable, yet just because the schools and corporations they wish to work for do not need their services at the moment is no reason for them to feel consigned to the tenth pit of hell. The same is true for you, whether you have a Ph.D. or not.

An employer, after all, is merely an intermediary between your efforts and the customer—the student buying the education of which your English lit course is a part, for example, or the family buying the software into which you put your engineering and design efforts. If employers are unavailable to serve as vehicles for your promise, connect with your customers in another way. Write a book. Start a consulting practice. Put one of your recitals on tape.

You have done all this work to develop competence and a point of view, to cultivate your abilities. Don't give up on fulfilling your promise when you are so close to success. Just because clients are not hiring you on a long-term contract does not mean you are not talented and valuable. Find a vehicle for bringing your promise all the way to us. Package your talent differently. Imagine a different way to be paid.

Remind yourself of your vision. What do you see that others don't? How can you package your ideas in an original way? Who else could you bring your work to? The answers to these questions often mean the difference between doing work that thrills and supports you and doing work that depresses you.

DOES THIS MEAN I WILL HAVE TO SELL? This sounds suspiciously as if you will have to sell your own work, and you may be philosophically opposed to selling or convinced that you can't do it. Hustling people, you may say, is not my forte.

Relax about the hustling. You don't need to push anyone into anything. You don't need slick sales pitches, power closing moves, or high-gloss Italian shoes.

You need two things. First, you need to remember that it's not our job to seek you out, whether you are a brain surgeon, a watercolor artist, or a software engineer. It's your task to fashion your vision into an appealing, compelling offer. If you don't bring your vision all the way to us, you can't expect to be paid.

Second, you need to understand that your vision is actually not that difficult to carry. If you are working on articulating your vision, you simply need to express yourself. People will pay you enormous sums if you can learn to do this well.

Consider the work of Michael, a highly successful sports photographer. Michael likes to sell customers photos that he has already taken, known as stock photos, more than he likes to work on assignment, because he can make more choices when he calls the shots. When he shoots at a sporting event, he chooses which athletes to photograph as well as the angle, timing, and exposure of each shot. When he stages a photo shoot he chooses the models, their clothes, the props, the angle of the shots, the lighting, the time of day, and the location. He also decides which sport to shoot.

"When I shoot assignments, the clients usually have a pretty complete idea of what they want, and I feel as if I'm on remote control. When I shoot stock photos, I do better work, because I don't have their constraints."

Michael's stock photos have earned him an outstanding income for years. They have afforded him and his wife the opportunity to design and own a luxurious and architecturally stunning home. What are his clients paying him such large sums for? They are really paying him for calling all the shots. In essence, they are paying him for his self-expression.

Don't let a fear of selling stand between you and the people who can use your work. This is a recipe for insecurity and a poor income. Instead of dwelling on whether your work falls into the category of selling, focus on bringing to clients work that reflects your unique expression.

You are most compelling when you are expressing yourself, and clients will pay handsomely for self-expression.

Keep Your Appointment with the Universe

The third part of cultivating your talent is to remember as you take the first two steps that you do not control the planet. You are not cranking your way through a math problem. You are orchestrating. You are cultivating.

Four years into launching a Silicon Valley start-up, the lead founder called a meeting of his board of directors intending to give up on the company. Customers to date had placed only single orders for small quantities of the firm's product, and he was convinced that they could survive no longer without a large long-term contract. He was tired of working for no income. He was tired, period. As he informed his board of all this, the tone of the meeting was understandably bleak.

After listening for a while, one of his partners offered a single comment: "I have made worse investments than this." He then offered to put another $50,000 into the company. It was his belief, he explained later, that people could use the firm's product; they just did not know about it yet. The tone of the meeting shifted. The other capital partners agreed to additional investments. The company carried on.

For two months, nothing happened. Then a customer who had purchased ten to twenty units at a time phoned with another order. Asked if he would consider a long-term contract, he said no, just another single order. This time, though, he ordered 1,500 units. The firm earned about $1 million profit on the order, which kept them in business and put them on the map. Four years later, the founders sold the firm for slightly more than $200 million.

The lead founder did not secure the long-term contract he wanted. Ask him, though, and he'll admit that what he received was more than acceptable. Months after the buyout, the entrepreneur summed up the key to his success this way: "Don't just try—do it."

Yet this isn't what he really did. His sound bite makes it

seem as if he kept at some form of master plan when in fact the firm's darkest moment developed because he was trying so hard to just do it and keep at it that he almost did himself in. Had he clung to the idea that the firm needed a contract by a certain date, the firm would have folded at that board meeting. There would have been no multimillion-dollar buyout, no satisfaction, no product helping people.

"She kept at it." That's how success stories are often told after the fact, when success is plain for all to see. As advice, however, "Keep at it" implies that accomplishment always proceeds in a straight line. It doesn't. Nor do accomplished people always know exactly where they are going. "Keep at it" implies that you can do something to make success happen to you. Sometimes in fact you can't. On the contrary, sometimes all the forces are in place, and you must simply do nothing with every ounce of energy you possess.

Sometimes the point is not to keep at something. Back off instead. Don't do it. Just let it happen. Sometimes the power is in having some touch. Sometimes there is nothing to do other than stay out of your own way.

Cultivating your talent is not a linear task. Sometimes what you really need to do is take refuge in your work and stay open, literally and figuratively. To reap all the rewards of being accomplished, sometimes you need to keep your appointment with the universe even though you have no idea where the meeting is being held.

SO DO I TAKE RESPONSIBILITY FOR MY SUCCESS WITH MY WORK, OR IS IT REALLY OUT OF MY HANDS? As you work on making your promise pay off, you will surely receive some unanticipated gifts. You may discover a talent for public speaking that you had no idea you possessed. You may set yourself up for a long search, then unexpectedly find that the firm you want to work with has an opening for a person with precisely your skills and point of view.

Perhaps you hoped to find twenty investors willing to put $3,000 apiece into your bike-manufacturing venture, but the third person you call proposes to put up the entire $60,000. The director you meet may not want the screenplay you have completed, but he will pay you to write the other one you have in mind.

In these cases you must let go of your original plan, accept the gift, and move gratefully, humbly, and joyfully on. You are making good on your promise.

As you work, you may also experience moments when you'd be willing to exchange a body part for just one unanticipated gift.

You may struggle a long time to catch a glimpse of your promise. Your talent may not develop as fast as you would like. Customers may not line up at your door in the numbers you expect or need. Your lead investor may drop out.

You may want a publishing contract. Instead, maybe you'll get an agent. You may want a payday, and instead you'll get more work. Despite your best efforts, life will not turn out according to your plan.

What do you do in these instances? If you live by the advice to "keep at it," chances are excellent that you will eventually do one of two things: you will become discouraged and quit, because your persistence is not producing success as you have defined it, or you will try to pressure people into doing what you want. In the former instance you'll be like the entrepreneur, on the verge of missing out on the very success you desire. In the latter instance, you will scare your clients off.

Neither of these responses will help you earn the cash, security, and fulfillment you seek.

You have another option, though. If you can simply know that events are sometimes out of your hands and accept that without giving up your commitment to make good on your promise, you can find a more fruitful way to proceed. Consider that your current difficulty, as painful and uncomfortable as it may be, is exactly what you need to obtain the profits, satisfaction, and connection you seek.

Consider that the difficulty may actually be one of the gifts. If you can think in terms of cultivating and cradling your promise instead of either riveting yourself to a goal or completely abandoning it, new possibilities will appear.

You must take responsibility for catching a glimpse of your promise, leaning on your talent, and bringing your expertise all the way to us. You must be no-turning-back committed to making your promise pay off. You must honor the part of you that says you will not be denied.

Yet in the same moment you must also be willing to surrender your preconceptions. You must consider that your promise is coming forth, but that it is just not happening at all the way you expected. This requires that you give up ideas about how and when you thought your success should happen, that you give up the notion that you can know in advance how a particular stretch of life will unfold, and that you give these up more than you thought you would have to. You must be willing to admit that these preconceptions and expectations are not essential to you, and find a new way to fulfill your promise. You will probably have to do this more than once.

If you can be dedicated yet open, you put yourself in position to seize opportunity more readily and to spend less time recovering from misfortune. If you can develop the intellectual dexterity to take just the right amount of responsibility for your success, you can accomplish a lot in life.

What do you do? You may think it will be years before you will make money as a concert pianist, if at all, but you must start down that path nonetheless and figure out how to make it pay as you progress.

You may have constructed a budget and a timeline for developing a theft-proof bicycle, and you may be wrong about both. If so, you must improvise. Maybe the bike needs a stronger design before it can take off.

Those night courses in the registered nurse's program just increased in tuition. You must remain calm, pay for them anyway, and figure out a way to come up with your rent before the first of next month. Maybe you can secure a better-paying interim job that is closer to your real interests.

You may have put all sorts of effort into that first screenplay, but if it is simply not selling, you must not lose your nerve. You must write a more compelling script. Perhaps you will learn something in writing the second script that will enable you to sell the first one for ten times what you originally thought it might command.

Cultivating talent requires you to stay loose. Finding work that fits you means taking responsibility for fulfilling your promise but surrendering your expectations when life does not go according to plan. Remember that some of this is out of your hands.

How much money should I bank before I switch to work that fits me? And how do I know when to make the switch? At some junctures of life, shifting to work that fits your talents presents little financial difficulty. If a job as a physical therapist, a guidance counselor, or a semiconductor plant manager will help you develop your talent, for example, and if an employer offers to pay you enough every two weeks to cover your expenses, your bank balance is not so crucial and the decision to take the job can seem pretty straightforward.

At other junctures, however, finances may present a much greater challenge. If instinct tells you that you need to train in physical therapy, guidance counseling, or semiconductor manufacturing, you may indeed need to take a cut in pay to develop your talent. If you are at the point where you need to start your own physical therapy firm, a private counseling practice for high school students, or a radically different kind of chip firm, you may be very uncertain about your immediate prospects for income.

As you see such a junction coming into view, pare down your expenses and pay off your debts as much as you can. Even if you don't see such a junction on the horizon, pare and pay off anyway, because if you are committed to fulfilling your promise, one will eventually appear.

If you are so inclined, consult a financial planner or set up a budget for the future. Be careful not to spend too much time, money, and effort on these activities, however. You are attempting to shift your life around, and often by trying to predict with scientific precision how much and where and when it will shift, you merely impede your own development and bring a lot of stress on yourself.

If you can have a year's expenses in the bank when you shift, great. If you can have two, that's even better. Note that the more you reduce your expenses, the sooner you can hit these benchmarks and feel comfortable about making your move. In all cases, you'll probably have to use some of your savings, which means your bank balance will go down.

As you husband your cash, continue to lean on your talents,

and also start flexing your imagination. Where can you set up a line of credit? From whom can you borrow? Where can you find people to invest in your work and ease your financial burden? What assets do you own that you can convert to cash? How can you cut expenses even further? Can you continue to work at your old job part-time as you start your more satisfying work? How can you package your work differently and bring it to a different set of customers?

You need not implement all of these financing ideas all at once. Start a list, though, and keep your imagination limbered up. Whether you want to sculpt for a living or build an apparel empire, you cannot predict the future, and you will most likely have to perform some financial improvisation from time to time. The more ideas you have in mind, the less the finances will distract you from your work, and the sooner you will be able to make your work pay off.

As for exactly when to make the break for a new horizon, the decision depends on a number of factors. Certainly your bank balance plays a role, though that role is much, much smaller than we often let ourselves believe, because one inspired financing idea can transform your entire fiscal picture and fund your work starting immediately.

How good are you at what you would like to do? Where are you in terms of feeling shortchanged about having to do the job you now have? The answers to these questions can also affect your timetable. In my experience the factor that overrides all others is whether you know deep in your gut that you can make your work pay off. When you have this bedrock confidence, take off.

Ultimately the best way to take care of your expenses is to start generating income at a craft that suits you in a fundamental sense. Ultimately the freedom to quit a job that no longer fits comes entirely from within.

HOW DO I DEAL WITH THE RISK? Consciously embracing work that fits you invariably entails risk. Leaning on your talent, taking responsibility for being paid, learning to cultivate your success—this can seem like an uncertain avenue to the profit, connection to others, and sense of self-worth that you seek.

The truth is, though, that you don't really have an attractive alternative.

Amy knows she is an artist, but she will never realize that potential while laboring over tax forms. This is not to say that being an accountant is incorrect or bad. It's just not her. Her choice seems fiscally prudent, but it is in fact unnatural and she pays a high price for being so unattached to herself. It seems as if she isn't starving, but in fact she is. Her spirit remains unexpressed, her talent lies undeveloped, and her vision of who she can be is left unfulfilled. Indeed she has no guarantee that the paycheck she values so highly will continue to arrive, and meanwhile she is leaving on the table all the money she could be earning as a successful artist.

Over time, no matter how much income Amy earns as an accountant, the pain of this small type of life will intensify because dreams do not die. They simply turn into regrets.

Robin, by contrast, is doing beautifully because she is cultivating her talent. She is practicing her art, teaching her art, and constantly learning more about her talent and how people value it. She has not yet had the breakthrough she wants, but she is still in the running.

If you give up on your promise, stop cultivating your talent, and instead opt for what seems like a certain paycheck, you sentence yourself to a life of pain. There's no middle ground between the risk and the pain, no place to hide out. It's an either/or choice.

When you fail to make good on your promise, you live small. Whether you hide out as an accountant who wants to paint, a housewife who wants to be a nurse, or a CEO who longs to teach third graders, you are unaccomplished.

If you dare to take the risk—to cultivate your talent, live beyond the numbers, and make good on your promise—you put yourself in a position to flourish. Amazing things can happen for you, as they have for my entrepreneur friend and for Michael the photographer.

Cultivating talent can seem like a complex task, but it is merely nonmathematical, and it is the way life works. The risk in finding and doing work that fits you is not so much that you may lose something essential to you as it is the simple willingness to embrace the unknown. Uncertainty aside, it is the right risk because the payoff is so rich.

Finding and doing work that fits you will secure you the self-esteem, the income, and the sense of connection that we all seek. This effort is a huge part of how you become accomplished as a human being.

In an important sense this effort is also how to become an attractive human being. Which would you find more interesting: being with someone who can articulate who she is in the world, or being with someone whose actions indicate that she can't say? Who sounds like a more intriguing partner in life: someone who's working on bringing forth his promise, or someone who's chronically bitter about living out a vision pressed on him by a short guy in a bow tie from Amherst?

When you glimpse your promise, start cultivating your talent at once. Grab the chance to bring that promise forth, because in a powerful and fundamental sense, that is who you are and that is who your partner wants to meet.

CULTIVATE YOUR TALENT

1. Drive over to the local university today and pick up information on courses you need to bring your expired teaching credentials up to date.

2. Start an idea file and buy the supplies you need to begin drawing your comic strip about the feline groundsman who camps out in your backyard every day.

3. What one thing do you think would most help your fledgling graphic design firm? Work on that instead of trying to estimate your chances for success.

4. Spend more time this week practicing the piano, and call the fellow who asked you three months ago about forming a band.

5. Change the subject to ice hockey when your uncle asks, for the eighth time in three months, whether your software has turned a profit yet.

6. Decline the invitation to the Super Bowl party and instead take a nap or go to the library and identify ten foundations that might help fund the documentary you are working on.

7. Start asking all of your friends and colleagues whether they know a literary agent who can help you sell your novels. Follow up every lead religiously until you find an agent.

8. Go over the product presentation that bombed last week and pull out the five lessons you learned. Having identified these gifts, declare the experience a success and fret about it never again.

TAILOR YOUR WORK TO FIT YOUR RELATIONSHIP

One Friday morning recently the phone rang at our house at 7:45 A.M. As I walked into the kitchen to answer it, I was pretty sure I knew who was calling, because only one person is likely to need to talk to Nancy or me at 7:45 on a Friday—the art student who takes care of Amanda from 8:30 to noon.

From the sound of Kristin's voice, I could tell she was sick. I wished her a speedy recovery and told her we would see her next week.

Just as I hung up, Nancy came into the kitchen wearing her dance leotards and sweatshirt. On Friday mornings in our house, Nancy normally goes to her favorite dance class of the week, and I go to the office. This day I had one meeting with a client, after which I was planning to write a section of this book that I had outlined the night before.

"That was Kristin. She's out with the flu," I told Nancy, and we knew one of us would have a morning that was not what we expected.

Work versus relationship—the choice all partners face far more often than they would like, a choice that appears to offer pain and frustration no matter which option they choose. How do you navigate over what looks like no-win terrain?

That Friday, Nancy went to class as scheduled and I took Amanda all morning. She sat on the floor next to my chair, coloring on copier paper, while I discussed the terms of a counteroffer with a client looking to sell his house. After I'd taken care of Fred, Amanda and I split a muffin and worked out on the play structures at the park up the street. We also ran an errand at the bank and picked up one of their royal blue balloons. To make up for the lost writing time, I worked late on Friday evening and went to my office on Saturday morning. Why did I do this? Because I am some great, self-effacing guy? Hardly. I did it for me. My relationship with Nancy enables me to express some of my deepest instincts about who I am and what I am here for. I don't want work or anything else to interfere with our rapport because I need that connection.

Consider what Nancy does for me. When I reach a tough juncture in a negotiation, I ask her opinion, not because I'm inadequate but because she has such impeccable instincts for helping me figure out what I think. When I have a problem with my writing, I go to her; she is my own in-house professional writing coach. She is so talented.

Consider what I have been able to help her do. I have helped her move away from being a director of communications for a banking association. I have helped her set up a schedule that enables her to write her own short stories and personal essays. Watching her grow is wonderful.

Together we are Amanda's parents, husband and wife, and partners in a life we navigate together. We have our moments of agitation, like any two human beings. Without each other, however, we would have neither our material success nor our bright prospects for the future.

Knowing how much Nancy enjoys dance class and how important a counterpoint it is to her writing, I would be foolish not to juggle my work around her preferences in order to keep our flow going smoothly.

Why should you tailor your work to your relationship? Because being in sync with your partner helps you remember who you are. You need the wisdom of the universe at work with you to fulfill your promise. You relax to try to find a vision of yourself. You cultivate your talent so you can be in touch with your promise and with other people. Your soul-to-soul connection with your partner is another place where you are in flow with the universe. Don't let work impede this connection.

What about your paycheck? The point here is not to ignore work but to tailor it. As you go about your work, keep in mind the following points.

Select a Boss Who Suits You

Joe used to manage a warehouse for a software firm vp who regularly ignored the suggestions Joe offered. In Joe's mind, the operation as the vp had set it up wasted warehouse space and money. Because of the operation's inefficiencies, Joe often had to work late, which cut into the time he could spend with his wife and daughter.

When he arrived home from work, Joe was often quite irritated at the events of the day and frequently spent a lot of time by himself, trying to work through his frustration. Many of his weekday and Sunday evening conversations with his wife, Sarah, were devoted to venting his resentment over the way the vp treated him. Having received but a single 3 percent raise in four years only added to his exasperation.

Finally Joe applied for a similar position with a different company and, to his surprise, was hired. His new employer gave him a 7 percent increase in pay and an office that was neat and clean. He also listened to Joe's suggestions about how to lay out the warehouse. When the lease on the building expired, Joe played a key role in finding a new site that was more conveniently located and better suited to the company's needs from a design standpoint. When the company decided to establish warehouses in other parts of the country, Joe was part of the group that attended to the task, and his opinions were valued highly.

What does Sarah say about Joe's new job? She says she feels as if she has her husband back.

The boss. He or she will not actually be in your relationship. It will only seem like it. Over dinner. While getting ready in the morning. Looking back on the week. Planning the week ahead on Sunday night. The boss will show up in all sorts of places.

Whether you work for an employer, with partners, or on your own with your clients, the person you work for is a big issue, and the questions to ask are simple: Is this person enhancing your life and your work, or is he impeding you? Is she enabling you to do work you want to do? Is she giving you room to breathe as a human being?

If your clients don't respect and value you, they will cause you aggravation, and both you and your partner will have to deal with it. If your boss sees employees as profit centers and not people who have children, feelings, talent, and dental appointments, she will anger you and you will bring your anger home. If your partners at work, your boss, or your clients don't have much of a life, they won't understand you wanting to have one, and the difficulties they cause you will be served at the dinner table on an all-too-regular basis.

Your boss will have a considerable impact on your relationship. Choose him carefully. And as your talent develops and your life unfolds, revisit your choice. If the truth is that the boss is more of a burden than a blessing in your life, start making plans to move on.

Customize Your Schedule

Your schedule also has repercussions for your relationship. Learning how to shape your schedule can make the difference between your partner feeling ignored and your partner feeling deeply cared for. Learn to give yourself room in some spots and to tighten up the fit in others.

When you absolutely have to work late, for example, be sure you follow up quickly with a gesture toward maintaining your rapport with your partner. Be home when you said you'd be home, or even earlier, if possible. Come home early the following day. Propose a Saturday date that's a bit more elaborate than the one you two had planned.

In setting your schedule, don't be afraid to use the entire week. If you really work well on Saturday mornings when no one else is in the office, then work on Saturday mornings, but come home at noon on Wednesdays or Thursdays so you can go to the zoo, take in a movie, or work in the yard with your family. If your wife needs a time and place to paint, come home early on Tuesdays to take care of the children, let her go to your office from three to nine, and have a meal ready for her when she returns. Let Sunday afternoons be her time as well. There's no law that says weekdays must be spent working or that weekends and evenings must be spent at home.

Sometimes people who seem important to your work will simply have to wait. A potential investor may propose that you meet next Monday. If you were planning to be away next Monday because it's your anniversary, you need to propose an alternative appointment time, no matter how inflexible you think this seems to him.

If you have to travel extensively or work extra hours over a certain period of time, discuss the schedule with your partner in advance and in detail. Edit your calendar with particular care during these times. Decline invitations to parties given by people you barely know. Resist turning on the television when you two are together. Organize yourselves so that when you are not working, you are deliberately nurturing your relationship, not just logging time in the same room.

Set up some specific ways to connect with your partner during the sprint. Propose a specific pattern of phone calls or a special weekly lunch appointment. Once the sprint is over, take some time off so you can make breakfast, prepare dinner, take care of the children, or generally be available for your relationship.

It's your calendar. Make it work for you and for your relationship. Stay loose about it. Be willing to shuffle. Just because you thought you would spend Friday morning at the office doesn't mean you have to in order to be accomplished.

Work with Your Own Fabric

Tailoring your work to your relationship also requires that you catch a glimpse of your promise, lean on your talents, and figure out new ways to serve your customers.

If you neglect the cultivation of your talent, you could end up feeling stuck in a job that suits neither you nor your relationship and powerless to do anything about it. I'm a marketing consultant for General Motors, the thinking goes, or I'm a secretary at O'Connor Hospital. I have to be here when they tell me to show up, and I have to do what they say, or else I'll be out of work.

Nonsense.

If you commit yourself to catching a glimpse of your promise, all sorts of interesting possibilities may appear. Perhaps you will decide to become a home improvement consultant, start a design firm, or apply for a different job at the hospital where you now work. Such a shift in your work could transform your entire experience.

By putting in the time to develop your talents, you not only give a more interesting arc to your work. You also make yourself more valuable to employers, clients, and partners at work. Being valuable means you will probably earn more money. The extra funds will allow you and your partner to purchase some time together, whether it's for dinner at La Luna or for a month in Spain.

Being valuable also means you will probably have more clout. Clout means you can have more of a choice about the people you decide to work for. It also means that those you work for will take your opinions, your advice, and your life more seriously. They will make larger allowances for your scheduling needs. You will thus have greater flexibility for weaving your work and your relationship together in an acceptable way.

If you are beginning to feel that the sprint is never going to end, pause in your efforts to tailor your schedule and consider whether a larger adjustment is in order. You need not necessarily go to work for yourself. Just understand that the ability to tailor your work rests to a large extent in your own hands. When you are working on your promise, tailoring is not that difficult, because you own the body of work.

Guidelines for Tailoring Your Work

You must compromise, we are often told, to fit work and relationship together. Join me in a life rich in trade-offs, the message seems to be.

Have a different mind-set instead. Don't compromise—improvise. Having an exquisite life together means growing and sharing your experience, not withstanding and minimizing an endless string of losses.

Talk to each other. Watch your messages. Proceed deliberately. Remember Rome was not built in a day. Both work and relationship add dimension to your life. Your life will not be complete with just one, because you are capable of both.

WHAT IF WE ARE JUST STARTING OUT? In other words, what if your boss is a pain? What if he sets your schedule in concrete and tells you exactly what to do all day? What if you have no idea what your promise is, and you can't quit because you need the money?

In such a case you and your partner can acknowledge that this is your situation, then begin trying to catch a glimpse of your promise. Everyone begins somewhere. Be supportive of each other. Maintain your soul-to-soul connection. Keep looking for opportunities and ways to fit your work a little more comfortably into your life.

In addition, remember that ultimately you are the boss: everything you do is your choice.

I HAVE CHILDREN SO I CANNOT TAKE THESE RISKS. WHAT CAN I DO INSTEAD? You may feel that because you have children you cannot afford the risks and effort involved in doing work that is true to you. While this viewpoint may make you feel that you are placing a high priority on your children, you are actually doing them a disservice.

Surely you want your children to be complete human beings, to make the most of their talents. But how will they know how to do that if they do not learn it by watching you do it? Again, tailor the work, don't abandon it.

"I would like to develop my talents further," says Toni, "but I can't because I have kids."

If Toni remains a grocery store clerk and never dares to put her talents as a scientist to use—she has a Ph.D. in physics from one of the leading programs in the country—the message she sends her two daughters about how to use their talents will not help them grow. She need not drop everything and jump into launching a cutting-edge genetic research company. Yet some small step would surely boost her self-esteem and at the same time show her daughters how to cultivate their talents.

Talent needs to be developed. Children need to be raised. Part of your task as an accomplished human being is to create a way to do both.

SHOULD MY PARTNER TAKE THAT NEW JOB, AND SHOULD I SACRIFICE MY JOB IN THE PROCESS? The real question here is what does the job do for the life the two of you want together? If it just pays the bills, it's not a particularly substantial opportunity. If you two can conceive of this turn of events helping both of you become more accomplished, then the job deserves your consideration.

MY PARTNER WORKS TOO MUCH. WHAT CAN I DO? Have a soul-to-soul discussion. Let him know you are more interested in your relationship than in your net worth and that you are prepared to be radical about money. Let him know that you are willing to give up stuff, like houses, cars, and clothes, and to change the patterns you have developed—both working late, spending the weekend reading the paper, and so on—in order to move back into sync.

If you are on the receiving end of this proposition, take a long look at making the changes your partner is advocating. Perhaps the problem is that you think and talk too much about work. Maybe you spend too much time there. Perhaps your partner thinks you are not spending enough time together or you are not pulling your weight at home. Whatever the case, listen up and navigate with soul, or be prepared to create a marriage of the spirit all by yourself.

TAILOR YOUR WORK TO YOUR RELATIONSHIP

1. Direct the discussion away from your work when you phone your partner while away on a work trip. Talk instead about the lunch your partner had with his mother, his day at work, the children's dental appointments, your plans to paint the garage this weekend, or other topics that locate you specifically in the life you share.

2. Ask from time to time—every few weeks perhaps—how your partner feels about the schedule you two keep. If adjustments seem to be in order, make them.

3. Leave the office briskly instead of ruminating for twenty to thirty minutes every evening about what you need to do tomorrow.

4. Instead of letting worries about work invade your time together, develop the habit of being confident that you will complete your work in excellent and timely fashion.

5. Determine what work-related issue stresses you out the most. Then do something about it.

6. Eliminate "crunch mode," "crashing on a deadline," and other collision-based phrasing from your vocabulary.

FIND WORK THAT FITS YOU AND YOUR RELATIONSHIP: BE ACCOMPLISHED

Does aiming for a blend of work and relationship mean that you necessarily have to compromise your work? No. Fitting your work to your relationship is not a question of settling for less. It's a matter of expanding your definition of what it means to be accomplished.

After all, you have all this talent.

And your partner is the person who is creating life with you. She is taking the time to have a soul-to-soul discussion with you. She is taking a stake in your work. She is thinking about the messages she transmits. She is doing her best to stay in sync with you. She is cultivating her talent so she can grow and bring you along on her journey. No doubt life is not perfect, but if you stop to consider what's going on, you can see that it's pretty rich.

Tailoring your work to fit your relationship is not a compromise. It's the deal of the century. All it requires of you is some logistical ingenuity and the willingness to apply yourself fully to the task of earning a living

So don't adjust because you ought to. Do it because you understand the benefits, and because you know that you can.

P R A C T I C E

1. What messages about your talent do you receive from your boss, customers, or partners at work? Do these people support your talent and express an interest in your ideas?

2. How does what you do compare to what you think you can do and who you think you are?

3. Name five problems you see in the world and devise solutions to them. Is there any work in these situations for you? Think big. Assume you have resources at your disposal.

4. Write a letter with three sections. First, describe the work you would do if you knew it would turn out well, if money was no object, and if you were sure you'd never fail. Next, write down all of the reasons why you cannot accomplish what you just described. And finally, explain why those reasons cannot really hold you back, and speculate about how you could establish your vision.

5. List ten small steps you could take toward realizing your promise. Begin with one step.

6. Name four ways to lean on your talents more heavily. Try one.

7. Identify the likely customers for work that suits you. How could you bring your promise to them—by establishing a firm, perhaps, or organizing a television show or taking a different job? How could you reach a greater number of people with your work? How could you increase sales twentyfold?

8. Think of a time when work did not go the way you wanted and yet ultimately provided you with more rewards than you'd have received had you gotten your way.

9. Given the work that you and your partner currently do, do you think you are headed for a lopsided relationship, as that term was described in Chapter 3?

10. Give your boss, your partners at work, or your clients a performance review. Are they making extra demands on your time or causing you anxiety that impairs the life you have outside work? If so, can you improve the situation by changing your behavior and making some polite requests of them, or do you need to look for new people to work with?

11. Sit down with your partner and examine your schedule.

Do your working hours dovetail with your need to exercise, relate, rest, and be with your children? Experiment here. Use all seven days, as well as all twenty-four hours. Do you need to exercise at 7:00 A.M. or at noon? Are both of you receiving the time you need to work—that is, not just to collect a paycheck but to develop your talents? Have you incorporated time for your date? Would it be better for you and your family if you worked from 6:00 A.M. to 2:00 P.M.? How should you split the cooking chores? Revisit these questions every season.

Circuit Training

Select an activity from this list:

- Finish cleaning up the house, garage, or car.
- Lay in a fresh supply of pens and paper at your house. Recycle ruled or graph paper—the lines constrict your spirit and imagination. Toss your pencils and black pens. Buy pens in your favorite colors.
- Go to the library, check out four books on four different subjects, and read them.
- Stamp your work space with your signature somehow— rearrange the furniture, or frame a favorite photo or sketch and hang it where you can see it.
- Go for a long run, swim, or walk, or take a longer yoga class.

Applied
Fundamentals

6 Quit the Fear-Based Lifestyle

Enlightened Answers to Difficult Financial Questions

The key to using money to nourish your relationship, bank-book, and soul is to practice money's fundamentals at every turn. Not just occasionally or when you clearly recognize the course you should take. Be deliberate, aware, articulate, and accomplished *all* the time, especially when you are confused about how to proceed. Practice the fundamentals when they feel right, and practice them when they don't. By employing these basic principles routinely, you and your partner will put yourselves in position to enjoy a highly evolved standard of living.

As you two reach for a more advanced life together, you will surely confront some difficult financial choices. If you turn to the customs of personal finance for guidance at these junctures, your anxiety will often mount, financial success will frequently elude you, and you can easily end up struggling with a life that in many ways feels standard and poor. By applying money's fundamentals instead, you can quit living a fear-driven life and achieve a wealthier existence.

Here are some common crossroads where the fundamentals can serve you particularly well.

How Much Debt Should We Take On and When?

Rick and Tina rented out their first home and, with the help of two mortgages, purchased a second one. Their hope was to capture the appreciation on two houses instead of just one. Unfortunately, the economy did not perform according to plan.

In the year following the purchase of the second house, home values dropped about 15 percent and stayed there. Two years later, a decline in the defense industry cost Rick his job, which left them with little income. After seven months Rick still had not found a new job, and the couple faced a thicket of financial problems: the equity in the second house had evaporated, because the house was now worth about $5,000 less than the mortgages they had relied on to buy it; they were $28,000 behind on their mortgage payments and taxes; and their savings eroded with every week that passed.

When I met with them, the air in their home was thick with tension. Neither Rick nor Tina could stay seated for more than a few minutes at a time. Rick would jump up to look out the window or to dig up some document that we didn't really need. Tina would bolt off to straighten up the coffee table or wipe the kitchen counter, declaring that she was sick of the whole mess.

Whenever Rick spoke, he tried to sound casual and relaxed, but many of his comments ended with statements like "and that's how we put ourselves in this hole." When he wasn't berating himself, he was wrapping his arms tightly across his chest or clenching his fists.

The couple eventually sold the second house, using some of their savings to pay off the overdue taxes and the two loans. They moved back into their first home, Tina resumed her nursing career, and Rick worked on some small, short-term projects for local firms.

Their story could easily be cited as a vivid reminder to stay away from debt at all costs, and that is indeed the customary advice given by many so-called experts. Yet if you slow down and think a bit more deeply about debt, you will see that it is not without redeeming value.

For starters, people go into debt to pay for some genuinely important expenses—college education, for example, or surgery. There are times when negotiating a loan is a most intelligent way to live.

Additionally, the reality is that we are all in debt, not in the sense of having outstanding credit card balances, but in a larger sense. The dollars are all promissory notes, and they are worthless unless everyone agrees they are valuable, so we are literally indebted to each other for that support of the currency. The wholesale condemnation of debt that many experts call for is inappropriate and naive, because without debt we'd still be bartering for goods and services, and civilization would still be operating at a crude standard of living.

If you succumb to custom and develop a fear of borrowed funds, you impair your own standard of living and perpetuate the struggle with money in two ways. First, the fear of borrowed funds limits your life in those instances where, for whatever reason, you have indeed taken on a debt. The notion of having this monster, this debt, in your household devours huge portions of your attention. As Rick and Tina's case demonstrates, when you let this fear roam the house, you are miserable and rapport with your partner is an afterthought at best.

Fear of debt also tends to cause you to deny yourself use of an honest vehicle for financing some expenses that would genuinely contribute to your life. If you really feel that you would profit from completing college, for example, yet for financial reasons you decide not to return or to settle for a watered-down version, you hamstring your own growth. If you have a good idea for a cookie company yet refuse to consider a loan to establish it, the cookies and the connection, esteem, and cash that they would generate, may never be realized. Good ideas typically appear before they generate income, not after.

When you deny yourself these sorts of opportunities to contribute to your own life, your promise languishes unrealized. Saying no to an opportunity just to avoid borrowing is no different from going to work as an accountant just because it seems to pay better than teaching. It is living for the bucks, and living small.

You and your partner cannot afford to take the customary stand on debt. At some point in your life together you will most likely need a loan to bring yourselves forth in the world, and you cannot afford to be deeply distracted or small about it. Instead, you need to move on and, among other things, pay off the loan and not put your rapport on hold in the meantime.

Minimizing Debt

Do you live in fear of having to borrow funds? Do you find yourself living in fear of the debts you already shoulder? Exactly when is borrowing appropriate?

The key to handling debt in an enlightened manner is to think in terms of being accomplished. This fundamental will help you minimize debt in three ways.

First, focusing on being accomplished will help you minimize the amount you borrow. Will the expense you propose to fund enhance your ability to bring forth your promise as a human being? If so, you borrow. If not, you pass.

By this standard, Rick and Tina should have rejected the idea of buying that second house because the loans they signed up for did not serve them. They did not borrow to enhance their life. They borrowed to purchase a piece of real estate in hopes that it would someday yield cash. This expenditure did not in any way enhance their esteem and intimacy or develop their ability to support themselves and connect with others. It was pure financial speculation. Even if they had earned $50,000, they would have reaped little genuine upside.

New bone china, new Armani golf shoes, a new cigarette boat—these items do not relate to your command and richness as a human being. Adoption expenses do, as do expenditures related to work that fits you. Every loan you consider taking on should be judged on its ability to bring forth the promise within you. By being true to this standard, you will keep your borrowings to a minimum.

Second, concentrating on being accomplished will help you pay off debts you already have and conceive of ways to pay off loans you would be wise to undertake.

Rick and Tina's problem in the aftermath of their unpleasant experience was that they had not been leaning on talents or cultivating customers in their work. They had no work in progress that would soon yield a sizable income, and this reality only prolonged their cash flow difficulties and increased their anxiety.

When you are focused on work that fits you, you have more flexibility about your income. When an expense arises and a loan seems wise, you can immediately start thinking of ways to bring your promise to more people or to improve its value. This will enable you to acquire the funds to pay off the loan.

The third benefit of focusing on being accomplished is that you feel good about yourself when you are doing work that fits you, and your concern about your obligation recedes. It does not dominate your mind. The work of becoming accomplished realigns your perspective and minimizes the impact of the loan on your life. You can be intellectually available to meet your partner for lunch or to meet your wife-to-be for the first time.

Naturally, you still have to pay off any debt you owe, but this way it will not consume you. You are not that debt. You are much more than that, individually and together. When you remain focused on recognizing your promise and cultivating your talent, you keep your mind free. This allows you to conceive of a way to earn more income, to free yourself to do the work, and to stay together in the process.

SHOULD WE INVEST $25,000 IN MUTUAL FUNDS OR DIRECTLY IN THE STOCK AND BOND MARKETS?

> *Rethink risk. If you're a boomer, you have plenty of time to recover from stock market setbacks—maybe two decades more than previous generations. Don't get too prudent: invest in equities, and don't throttle back too soon.*
>
> —Stephen M. Pollen and Mark Levine, *Worth,*
> January 1995

Bonnie thinks that she and Dusty should invest their savings as well as their retirement accounts in the stock market. Dusty thinks that at age forty-five no more than 40 percent of their assets should be in the stock market, with the remainder split between relatively low risk mutual funds and bonds.

Investment risk is a frequent source of friction between

Bonnie and Dusty. As the advice quoted above suggests, however, engaging in this discussion is seen as a virtual necessity, friction or no friction. Pointing to a chart showing the stock market's favorable performance since 1926, the experts frequently tell us that we cannot afford not to be invested there and urge us to be aggressive. The choice between mutual funds, stocks, and bonds is a source of debate, like the choice between prime rib, sirloin, and T-bone. Taking some investment risk, though, has become a custom that is all but unchallenged.

If you don't rush into picking one of the items off this menu, however, two interesting questions surface. The first is this: how will any of these investments help you become a more accomplished human being? The answer is that they won't.

They may help you generate some cash, and you may plan to use that cash for a most worthy aim, such as your son's college education or the purchase of a bed-and-breakfast inn when you retire, and you may envision feeling fulfilled about this development. In the investment itself, however, there is no fulfillment. You must do something satisfying with the funds in order to be fulfilled. Even if your investments yield 20 percent annual gains for years to come, the act of sending your funds to Fidelity or Merrill Lynch and then waiting does nothing for your sense of connection with those you serve, your rapport with your partner, or the cultivation of your talent. The customary investment vehicles do nothing meaningful for your competence as a human being.

This realization leads to the second question: is there someplace you could put your funds where the payoff would be more substantial? Yes—work that fits you. Couples like Dusty and Bonnie needlessly perpetuate the struggle with money and bring friction and anxiety into their relationship because they focus on taking the wrong risk. They also forgo an investment that could pay off five to five hundred times better than anything Fidelity or Merrill Lynch will ever have to offer.

Missing Out on the Risk That Pays Best

Assume that in the ten years after graduating from law school, I opted for a customary investment program. Assume that my salary rose, despite the ups and downs of the Bay Area property market, a healthy 10 percent annually, from $20,000 to $47,000 during that decade. Assume, even though the cost of living in San Francisco rose 37 percent in that period, that I kept my expenses level, thanks to superhuman self-control. Assume that I also employed the superhero discipline to save my entire raise after state and federal taxes. Finally, assume that I earned 8 percent annually after taxes on my investments, an impressive return for a ten-year stretch.

My net worth at the end of the decade would have been about $90,000. A lot of people don't have ninety grand. This would have been a very respectable sum. Of course, if I had lived this life, I never would have met my wife, which means Amanda would not be here, either. Furthermore, I suspect that the miserly nature of this life would have depressed me deeply, and I am certain that this life would have prevented me from developing the income prospects and the competence that I possess today. I would not even have bought that exceedingly cool and exceedingly expensive leather jacket in year seven. I would have been strapped in too tight on a nonstop ride to $90,000.

Compare this to how I actually spent those ten years: I opened two IRAs and cashed in both prematurely, incurring the 10 percent penalty each time. I went $60,000 into debt to start my own firm, made some mistakes, learned to survive them, and learned to trust my instincts. I did not buy any stocks, bonds, or mutual funds, and I ended up with Nancy, Amanda, the leather jacket, and a net worth in excess of $250,000.

Not surprisingly, I am happy with my choice of investment. The fact that customary investments cannot provide you with the intangible rewards that money can yield makes sense once you stop to think about it. What few people acknowledge, however, is that these investment risks are not even a good way to maximize the financial return on your investable funds. Using them as a start-up stake or as a safety net for work that fits you is the best use of this capital.

Investing in the markets typically precludes taking the risk that can pay off best. If you are like most couples, you do not have the funds to invest in both the markets and work that fits you, so when you put your cash in the markets, your work necessarily remains unaccomplished, your bankbook suffers, and you have less of a sense of who you are to share with someone else.

As for your sense of self-worth, you must live with the message implicit in all customary investments: you are not talented enough to earn money on your own.

Risks You Don't Know You Are Taking

I'm not alone in thinking that investment risk is the wrong risk to take with money. Neil Simon, the Pulitzer Prize–winning playwright, when asked about customary investments and the advisers who advocate them, declared his philosophy: "I can make more money for me than they can make for me."

The story behind Simon's philosophy is instructive. "I've lost tons of [cash], more than millions," he claimed. Why?

"[The investments] didn't interest me. I can't go and read the numbers and ask all the questions. I'm too busy doing my thing."

One loss that his advisers steered him toward stands out. In the 1960s, Simon sold the rights to both *The Odd Couple* and *Barefoot in the Park* for a paltry $125,000. An accountant convinced him that the plays would never yield a larger return. As a result, Simon never earned a cent from the long-running *Odd Couple* TV series.

Simon's investment losses and the horrible advice he received on handling the rights to his plays underscore a second point about investment risk: the decisions made by people who are paid to think purely in financial terms are often a financial disaster.

I know of one disgruntled Fortune 500 executive who, unknown to any of his colleagues, committed the company to purchasing a $45 million piece of land that it did not need. Within months of this purchase, the land's value dropped 50 percent.

I know of another public company whose executives hired some consultants from a Big Eight accounting firm and never realized until it was too late that the lead consultant had defrauded them out of $200,000.

You may say that the risks of cultivating your talents successfully seem scary to you and that you are more comfortable with standard investment risks, but in fact you have no idea when you invest in the markets what risks you are taking. Like Simon, you do not have time to read all the documents, meet all the people, and weigh all the information associated with the bonds, stocks, or mutual funds you purchase.

Investment risk is hardly the user-friendly experience that the brokers who sell it want you to think it is. It actually perpetuates your struggle with money but not just because it precludes the possibility of securing money's intangible rewards. Investment risk rarely pays off as well as work that fits you, and quite possibly it will not pay off at all.

Loftier Returns

Where do you have your funds invested? Which risk are you taking with them—one that can pay off or one that can't? Do you anxiously watch the financial pages, feeling that you are at the mercy of unknown and fickle forces? Do you hope the market performs the way you want, and try not to think about how dismal your prospects will look if it doesn't?

When discussing investments, you and your partner need to proceed deliberately. Don't be quick to conform to custom.

Be aware. Listen to the self-defeating message that flows from the act of using your funds in a way that fails to cultivate your talents.

Most of all, think in terms of being accomplished when you make investment decisions. Consider the return on talent that Neil Simon's plays have generated. Recall the wealth that Michael and the entrepreneur mentioned in Chapter 5 have orchestrated for themselves. Think about Nancy, Amanda, and my leather jacket.

You and your partner will profit from ignoring what you hear from Dean Witter and the *Wall Street Journal*. Instead of flirting with investment risk, put your funds in a savings account and go to work. Even if you have yet to identify work that fits you, you cannot afford to lose your savings while trying to catch a glimpse of your promise. Once you see the course you wish to pursue, you will be pleased that you have this capital backing you up.

The advertisements and advice that swirl around you will make it sound as if your capital will rot in the bank. Actually, it's performing an incredibly valuable service by financing the risk you and your partner need to take to evolve as human beings. Work is the only place your dollars can really pay off with income, fulfillment, and self-esteem, because that's where you tap into your talents.

You can argue that you lack talent, but as we discussed earlier, you will lose.

How Much House Should We Buy?

Jim was ready to buy a starter house even though he and Rachel could barely afford it. When they showed up for an initial consultation at the clinic, however, I discovered that purchasing a house was going to challenge more than their finances.

Jim wanted to talk about condos, one-bedroom homes, and fixer-uppers. Rachel said virtually nothing during our meeting. He was quite interested in understanding the benefits of having me represent them. She did not seem comfortable with even being in the room. The only time she seemed to relax a bit was when I recommended that they postpone buying any property whatsoever.

Rachel did not strike me, during that meeting, as a woman transported by love. Jim was clearly driving them to this deal, and she was a most reluctant passenger.

Jim's desire to shoehorn the couple into homeownership was not a well-considered idea, but he cannot bear the entire blame for his enthusiasm. There is a tsunami of cultural momentum that carries couples toward buying homes. The tax code gives you an interest rate deduction, a tax-free exchange, and a onetime exemption on part of the gain. Several million Realtors and the National Association of Realtors, the largest professional trade association in the world, launch a lot of advertising telling you that homeownership is good. There are approximately 70 million single-family homes in America, which means a lot of people you meet in life are sold on the idea of home ownership.

Houses are the cornerstone of the American Dream. They are also, however, along with work that does not fit you and saving for retirement, part of the Bermuda Triangle of personal finance. You and your partner can lose yourselves in your quest for a piece of this dream.

Looking for a house and a mortgage can take huge blocks of your free time. Months of it. Loan fees, commissions, inspection expenses, closing costs plus the purchase price, and later the mortgage, insurance, and property taxes can take huge chunks of your funds. Having to sell a home because of a reversal of fortune can consume still more time and more funds. As you try to figure out how big or how expensive a home you should live in, you can easily be swept into linking your self-esteem with your lot size.

Moving into a new home is often the occasion for a party, but in a festive yet complete way, it can basically kill your opportunity to fulfill your promise. It can inhibit your freedom to work and bring needless stress into your life together.

Don't let this happen to you and your partner. Buy yourselves a house when the time is right, but be deliberate about all aspects of the purchase. Leave yourselves plenty of spare cash so that you can finance work that fits you. Once you have purchased a house, if you have to choose between your work and the house, sell the house.

Keep in mind that the size of your den does not dictate the

quality of your life. If your partner is like Rachel, she will appreciate your perspective.

How Much Should We Save Every Month?

"Start by saving 1 percent of your take-home pay your first month; then increase the amount by half a percent each month. By the end of the year, you'll be socking away 6.5 percent per month."

Advice like this abounds in articles and manuals on personal finance, and the math that accompanies it always looks irresistible. If you save $90 a week starting at age thirty, you will have amassed $500,000 by age sixty-five. If you start at age twenty-five, you will have $700,000 by retirement.

If investment risk makes you nervous, a savings program can seem like a very compelling alternative. Work the job, stash the cash, duck the risk, and plan to get rich slowly.

To think that a savings program is without risk, however, is to miss the point about money. A savings program can eclipse your promise just as completely as an investment program can. The problem isn't only where you put the funds, it's the fact that you can become addicted to the program. You can develop the misconception that life will blossom for you if you will simply stick with the program.

Fixated on the need to make a deposit every week, you can talk yourself into denying the frustration you feel about keeping a job that fails to utilize your talents. Thinking that the sum you will have amassed by age sixty-five will make everything okay, you can demand that your partner engage in the same sort of self-denial, thereby upping the stress level in the household considerably.

If you let the program dominate your actions with money, you increase the chances that you will decline to take the risks of cultivating your talents and developing a vision of how you can serve people. The two of you have talents, but in demanding that you save above all else, the program denies you the income they could produce and effectively appraises the future value of your promise at zero.

By programming your savings, you and your partner tend to make life very linear, and you increase the likelihood that you will not find work that fits you, much to the detriment of your bankbook, your relationship, and your peace of mind.

Dreams That Are Worth the Investment

Are you and your partner on a savings program? Is that program bringing a Great Depression–type mentality into your household? Do you notice the two of you investing in yourselves very often, or not really much at all?

You need not settle for a cramped, linear life aimed at a savings objective. You can flourish and reap a wider range of rewards that includes a large net worth. Once again, the key is to focus on being accomplished in life. When you do, the natural place of savings in your life becomes clear.

Save when you can. Any savings account will do. Aim for two years' expenses, and when you amass that sum, aim to double the amount. Moving toward this objective will cut down on your time at the mall.

In conjunction with this savings effort, however, you must find work that fits you, and you must make your savings available to fund this work. If you need to put your savings efforts on hold because you are cultivating your talents and the work is not yet yielding any excess funds, so be it. If you need to rely on savings to cover expenses, that's fine. There are all sorts of ways to fund a work in progress: you can assemble a group of investors, you can borrow, you can secure a fellowship or scholarship, you can use savings. Do not feel bad if you choose to use your savings. You are investing.

Building a big bank account is not a linear activity. It is also much more than a financial affair. The payoff will be rich and it will arrive, but you must dare to lean on your talents and practice bringing your promise all the way to us.

Fourteen years into a banking career, Janice resigned her vice presidency, arranged for a student loan, and earmarked her savings for tuition to a bachelor of fine arts program at a local university. When asked why she was cashing in her savings and trading salary, benefits, and position for student life, she replied, "The way I see it, it's a fairly easy decision. If I am willing to give those things up, I get to pursue my dream. I have decided that my dream is worth the investment."

Your dreams are worth the investment, too. Make sure you put your promise ahead of your savings program.

How Do We Save for College Expenses?

I recently heard a financial reporter on the radio address the question of how to reconcile the need to save for a child's college education with the need to save for retirement. The reporter recommended that you act as if you are aboard a 747 that is about to crash: put on your own oxygen mask first, then help your child with hers.

Even if you choose not to view your daughter's college career as an airline disaster in progress, college expenses can cause you and your partner significant anxiety. Today many financial experts advise that you complete a worksheet that strings together present-day college tuition costs, an inflation rate, a rate of investment return, and a batch of other variables. You fill out the worksheet, throw the switch on your calculator, and frequently find yourself looking at numbers so large you assume the calculator has malfunctioned.

Jolted by this experience, you can easily fall into living a paint-by-numbers life, a life in which everything you do is calculated to produce the cash you need for your offspring's future. If you must stick with a horrible job because it pays well, fine. If you must spend less time with your spouse and less time with yourself so you can work overtime, that's life. Thanks to the worksheets, you can wind up with more savings for college, but less of a life for your family.

It is natural to be concerned about your child's future and to be willing to make sacrifices for her. You want to make sure she has the credentials to earn enough income so that she does not have to live in depression-type conditions.

If you move more deliberately here, though, you will see that there's an opportunity much larger than the worksheets let you know. Saving for college does not have to be an airline disaster or even a family ordeal. Instead, it can be an opportunity to contribute to the lives of everyone in the family.

Raising Accomplished Human Beings

Are you fearful that you will not be able to pay cash for your child's college tuition? In the back of your mind, though, is there some inkling that you will find a way to finance this expense, even though you don't at the moment know what it is?

You can build on that sense that there's an astute way to handle this challenge. Consider college funding costs in terms of being accomplished. This thinking will enhance your ability to educate your child in two ways.

First, this mind-set will shift your idea of what it means to build an educational trust for your child. Many people who set up a trust for a child create a legal vehicle into which they place cash or assets that the child can use to pay her expenses. By keeping in mind the need to become accomplished in life, you realize that instead of a financial fortress, you need to create a stock of personal mettle for this youngster. No amount of money—whether you give it to her or she earns it—will ever fortify her. To flourish in life, she needs to develop the ability to bring forth her promise, economic conditions notwithstanding.

As a parent, you can provide one of life's most valuable gifts by showing her a strong example of how to become accomplished in the work of living life. Four years of college is a wonderful gift, but ultimately that gift pales in comparison to the educational impact that you and your partner can have on your child. Others will supplement your educational efforts, but you and your partner carry the bulk of the load.

By thinking in terms of being accomplished, you realize that you cannot afford to work at jobs that are less than fulfilling under the premise that you need tuition money. Your pursuit of work that fits you is too important to your child.

In addition to adjusting your perspective, thinking in terms of money's fourth fundamental will also help you raise the funds to cover tuition, room, and board. As we have discussed, raising money is at root an act of imagination, and a highly developed imagination will serve you well in financing your youngster's higher education.

You may need to take out student loans. You may need to

apply for scholarships. You may need to drive to Yale or Purdue or the College of Southern Arizona or wherever your child wants to go and ask a financial aid person a lot of questions about loan programs and scholarships. You may need to make a list of wealthy individuals you know or know of, and arrange a private loan from one of them. To help your child realize her promise, you may need to find work that fits you, cultivate your own talents, and make your own promise pay off more than it has in the past.

There is no shortage of funds on the planet. By thinking in terms of being accomplished, you recognize more readily all the possible sources for the sums you require.

No matter how much cash you need to raise, you are not in the midst of an airline disaster. You have a lot of financing options at your disposal. Your child will attend college if she wants to, and you can cover the cost. She can become a highly accomplished human being, too, especially if you show her how.

How Can We Minimize Our Taxes?

"Why is this so hard?"

Exasperated, Chris leaned back in her chair and looked at me. As part of their retirement strategy, she and her husband, Keith, were trying to arrange a tax-free exchange. In plain terms, they were trying to sell a rental house they owned, buy an office building in the town where they planned to retire, and follow IRS guidelines along the way so the profit on the rental would not be subject to tax. The task was more consuming than they had anticipated.

They had spent several vacations looking for acceptable

retirement spots. They had spent the spring fixing up the rental and selling it. They had spent recent weeks looking at available buildings, consulting with their tax and investment counselors, and documenting their actions to satisfy the IRS.

Chris and I had spent the morning reviewing the purchase agreement on their new investment. Knowing that the IRS time frames for these exchanges are relatively short and that the couple would soon have to buy a property or pay taxes, the seller of the building they were targeting had rejected their last set of proposed changes to the contract.

When I asked Chris how Keith felt about taking the risk of buying the building with the contract as is, she said that her husband was fed up with the whole process, that he did not want to go forward, and that the exchange was now a sore subject between them. He had punctuated his position by refusing to come with her to our meeting.

"We have put all sorts of time into this," she continued. "At this point we get up, go to work, and muck around with this investment. It's all we do. There's no time for anything else. It's depressing, but I don't know how to avoid it."

The reason this was so hard for Keith and Chris was that they were letting taxes dictate their life. They went ahead and completed the exchange, and in doing so they were not alone. Every year Americans spend billions of dollars and countless hours trying to minimize their taxes. Tax avoidance is a growth industry. Countless couples purchase houses specifically for the tax break that interest rate deductions offer. Less, the tax experts tell you, is better.

Yet all the time and expense you devote to fencing with the tax laws can only net you small change. If you are in a 28 percent tax bracket and you come up with $2,000 in extra deductions in a year, you have saved yourself $560 in taxes. And

$560 really isn't that much. Neither, for that matter, is $5,000. Furthermore, consider what you frequently have to endure to come up with it: the reckoning, the small-minded mind-set, the distraction, the friction.

As for the more involved tax maneuvers like tax-free exchanges, the effort, the rules you must comply with, and the time and effort you must expend increase exponentially. Just ask Chris and Keith.

A Watercolor Versus a Deduction

Is tax avoidance a wise investment of your time and talent?

Be aware here. Don't ignore your taxes, but step back and look at yourselves.

On the standard calculations, do them and move on. Don't bother taking another Saturday to go through them again in the hope that you might find another $50 deduction. Don't bruise your brain digging for these small potatoes. This is not what accomplished people spend their time doing. Spend that time at the beach with your partner, going for a run, or working on your latest short story. If you spent that time on one watercolor painting, on one call to a customer, who knows how much that would pay off?

As for the more intricate maneuvers, the best advice is simple: don't start. The next best advice is this: don't keep going unless it's a simple transaction. Chris and Keith thought they were going to set themselves up for retirement. But retirement is twenty years away for them. What will change for them in the interim?

They started out with a rental property around the corner from their house. They exchanged this for a vacant office building two time zones away, plus a duplex located on a former gas station site. Somehow this seems to have become more complicated, not better. They could simply have kept the rental. Or they could have sold it and just paid the taxes.

Minimizing your taxes has become something of a national pastime. Before you take it up, consider: the time you pass with your taxes can never be retrieved.

SOCIAL SECURITY HAS BECOME A BLATANT RIP-OFF. HOW CAN I GET SOMETHING OUT OF IT FOR US?

No one likes to pay for goods or services they never receive. The fact that you have to pay thousands of dollars to the government, coupled with the very real possibility that you will never receive a single Social Security payment yourself, may upset you. Understand, however, that your anger may not all be directed at the government. Be aware of three points about sending off these dollars.

First, keep in mind that Social Security helps support your parents, your partner's parents, your aunts and uncles, and many others who have done a lot for you. If none of these people are here any longer, keep in mind that it supports the eighty-three-year-old man across the street or the woman who just retired as the librarian at the local junior high school. You and your partner are good people to support these folks. Your dollars are not being baled and burned.

Second, it is indeed entirely possible that your children will not receive any benefits from this fund. Teach them accordingly. Show them by example how to work their talents into a life that will support them. This will be among the most valuable lessons you can offer them.

Finally, render the amount of money you pay here insignificant to you. Yes, you pay your taxes, and Social Security is a burden you would rather do without if you are not going to benefit directly. But you have the capability to earn a large enough income so that paying Social Security will not affect your finances very much. You also have the capability to live a large enough life so that making this payment will not distract you.

Perhaps part of your anger over the inequity of the situation arises from the fact that you know you are too valuable to concern yourself with the relatively paltry amounts you must contribute to Social Security.

You have plenty to do and plenty you can do. Don't let small change ruin your concentration.

WILL WE REALLY BE THE FIRST GENERATION NOT TO DO AS WELL AS OUR PARENTS?

Teachers Insurance and Annuity Association manages hundreds of millions of dollars in retirement funds. In a recent ad in *Harper's* they posed the following question: "Your grandfather did better than his father. Your father did better than his father. Are you prepared to carry on the tradition?"

With as much political correctness as they could muster, the fund managers implied that it has become custom in the United States for children to have more cash in the bank than their parents, and that the measure of your life will be how well you conform to this custom.

Determined to measure up, you can redouble your efforts to minimize your taxes, buy a house to make sure you capitalize on rising real estate values, and serve yourself a full plate of investment risk. Spurred on by ads like the one mentioned above, you can swear off debt forever and set up a college savings program. Bent on accumulating assets, you can write your senator about how the impending inequity of Social Security goes against the free enterprise system.

The problem with all these moves, however, is that they are all no-talent moves: implicit in making them is the idea that you have to cling to the dollars you have because you have no way to earn any more; and by focusing your efforts on making them, you frequently fail to cultivate your talents, so that earning more dollars does indeed become difficult for you.

Together these moves put you and your partner on a set of railroad tracks that lead to a small and fearful life. You live in fear of not having enough cash. Boxcars full of people travel these tracks, frequently at high speed. They become what former labor secretary Robert Reich called "the anxious class."

BEYOND FEAR-DRIVEN LIVING

You and your partner do not have to consent, however, to letting these customs dictate and disrupt your life together. You can live more deliberately, decline to conform, and live more richly.

The fact is that people who bought houses and took jobs in the 1950s subsequently benefited from two favorable economic developments—rising home prices and rising wages. These forces enabled them to amass a sizable net worth. Whether they enjoyed a high standard of living is a completely separate question.

By contrast we now live in a period in which a thirty-year career with the same employer is unlikely. As for profiting from a tenfold rise in real estate prices, we'll have to see.

Now is a time, however, when two partners can reasonably expect an opportunity for the fulfillment that comes with developing their talents. It is a time when technology enables us to work without the constraints of a large organization, if that's the direction in which our work carries us. It is a time well suited for couples who understand that money is an instrument of personal evolution and that they can safely relinquish the fear of not having enough. They can use money to take life's most interesting risks and reap rewards that include cash but are not limited to it.

The fact is that your grandfather's life amounted to more than the size of his bank account. Same for your father, and same for you. Your family's standard of living is a result of being accomplished as human beings.

Those who challenge you to carry on the tradition of "doing better" than your elders are not conspiring to disrupt your life. Their thinking is simply not very evolved. They are doing the best they can, but there is no need for you to engage in any sort of intergenerational keeping-up-with-the-Joneses. This so-called tradition is in fact a myth.

When advertisements or advisers suggest you carry on the tradition, move deliberately. Examine closely what you are being asked to do. When you take the advice apart, you frequently find that you are being urged to make a no-talent move, and that the so-called advice is all myth and no substance. It simply fans your fears, nothing more. Once you realize this, you can then discard the advice and continue your efforts to become accomplished.

This type of calm use of the fundamentals will keep you from lunging into an attempt to compete with your great-grandfather's income. This approach will serve you and your partner well in other instances, too, because there are other powerful and potentially divisive financial myths that you also need to dismantle.

PRACTICE

1. Christmas, Hanukkah, birthdays, Mother's Day, Father's Day—how could you and your family arrange these events in the next year so that they will truly celebrate the people connected with them and soft-pedal the present-giving aspect? Perhaps you could concentrate on creating an elegant meal together, or go out to a really fine restaurant. Start a tradition of offering eloquent toasts and reminiscing. Buy some watercolors and try making some hand-painted cards.

2. Look at where your savings are currently invested. Who benefits from this arrangement and how? What message do these investments convey to you about your talent? How do they help you cultivate your talent?

3. Describe three ways in which you could raise $30,000 if you absolutely had to have the funds to survive, if you needed them to cover your daughter's tuition costs, or if you had a good idea for work and wanted to establish it.

Circuit Training

1. How is your exercise regimen progressing?

2. Describe in a paragraph how your education—in the Latin sense of bringing yourself forth—has progressed since you finished school. What sort of an example are you setting for your children? Name four ways in which you could devote money to your education.

3. Next time you receive an invitation to an event you suspect one of you would not enjoy, make sure you and your partner decline it.

7 Dismantling Five Money Myths That Can Drive You Apart

MYTH #1: RETIREMENT IS A NATURAL AND WORTHY GOAL

Marc was good on the saxophone. He graduated from a well-known school of music. He helped some friends produce an album, and he also cut one of his own. Today, though, he works for an insurance company, and there's no evidence of his musical interest in his home.

Instead of pursuing music, Marc opted for the security of becoming an adjuster for an established firm. He recently lost his job with that firm, however, and his compensation now includes health insurance with a much higher deductible, no life insurance, and no dental coverage for his wife or children. As for that man who was so interested in rhythm and composition, who didn't know anything about underwriting and actuarial tables, his wife and children have not really met him.

Asked whether he ever considered making a career out of his musical talents, Marc hesitates. He then explains that a career in music probably would have entailed a lot of travel, little security, and no retirement plan. As his mother pointed out to him, "There's no money in it."

How does he like the insurance work? "It's okay. The people are nice."

How does it compare to music? He smiles. "It doesn't."

It's easy to understand how Marc came up with the notion that he needed to concern himself with retirement. The message is everywhere. Robert Reich, the former labor secretary, wrote in *GQ*, "I know at your age you don't want to hear this, but it's never too early to think about retirement."

An investment manager, quoted in the *San Francisco Chronicle*, said, "If you are not saving for retirement, you are spending beyond your means."

Jackson National Life Insurance sends flyers to your doorstep urging you to invest with them "for a worry-free retirement."

"Imagine the possibilities," said one retirement brochure at the Charles Schwab office, "when your time is your own to spend the way you've always wanted."

The implication carried by this wave of input is that you need to log enough hours on the job and sock away enough investment funds so that, later on, you can "enjoy the good life" (Schwab's words). Captivated by this possibility, or fearful that ignoring this advice will spell doom, people like Marc do indeed live in the hope of reaching a worry-free retirement and a day when they no longer have to work.

The fact that retirement is culturally acceptable, however, does not mean it's a good idea.

Living Small

A deliberate look at the idea of retiring reveals two basic flaws. The first is that you compromise your present by trying to ride the rails that lead to retirement. This is no big surprise; the truth is spelled out right in Schwab's brochure: during the time between now and retirement, your time is not "your own to spend the way you've always wanted."

How does this happen? In fact, no one takes your time away from you. Retirement just gives you permission to waste it.

The underlying assumption of retirement is that life's big bonus will appear only when you have the money to retire. This being so, what you need most from each day is a constant predictable income so that you can invest regularly and build up the requisite bankbook.

What about doing work that compels you, expresses your spirit and talent, and could conceivably earn you enormous sums of money? The message between the lines of the retirement literature is that you probably are not talented enough to pull this off. Self-expression and wealth would be nice, but the retirement program calls for constant predictable income, not risk and reward. If you can simply obtain a paycheck for showing up when and where someone else says and doing what you are told, then stash some money in a mutual fund, you have achieved the day's primary objectives, and that should be good enough for you.

What about having time to be with your partner when you want, and sharing with him a larger expression of who you are? Again, nice idea, but for the aspiring retiree, constant predictable income and faithful investing are the day's objectives. Romance and intimacy will have to make allowances for your job.

With this heavy emphasis on regular income and faithful investing, retirement makes it easy to settle for less than what you want from each day. What's the danger in this? Your talent never develops. Even if you accumulate enough dollars to leave your job, retiring is a recipe for living small and settling for a life that's not your own. Just ask Marc.

As for the guarantee that, having ignored your talent, forgone a genuinely large income, and let your job and investment program dictate your actions, your retirement plan will compensate you by containing the appropriate sum when you reach age sixty-five—that document is nowhere to be found.

The Fallacy of the Worry-Free Future

The second problem with retirement is even more troubling than the first: the life that retirement appears to promise does not exist. A worry-free future in which you don't have to work?

Ask Noreen about that. She is trying to help her son as he starts a career and a marriage. She is trying to sell a nine-room house and find an acceptable two-bedroom condominium. She wonders whether to buy a new car, where to invest her money, and how to improve her income as a family therapist.

Or ask Janet. She has a divorced daughter living two time zones away with two children and no job. Janet's eighty-nine-year-old father recently fell and broke his hip. Much of Janet's net worth is tied up in an office building whose major tenant is about to move out.

A third client of mine is a seventy-five-year-old widower who owns a home and that's about it. He is trying to sell his home of thirty-two years and the attached land and buy a condo in a care facility. Paying his bills is a struggle each month, which tempts him into raising the price of the home. Once he sells, he wants to allocate his money so he can spend time with his children and grandchildren without burdening them financially.

Each of these people has a net worth of over $750,000. They are not unhappy with their lives, yet they hardly have "a worry-free retirement." All of them face plenty of challenges, and their assets neither insulate them from problems nor ensure that they will handle those problems well.

Anyone who thinks that problems disappear upon reaching age sixty-five and achieving a certain net worth will be sorely disappointed.

The Emptiness of Life Without Work

As for the part of the retirement bargain that promises a life without work, ask Glen how good a deal that is. He worked in high-tech corporations until just last year. He worked in large firms as well as small start-ups. After more than thirty years of challenges he genuinely enjoyed, he feels as if his life has hit sand. "I'm having trouble with it," he says of not having regular work that fits him.

Or ask Marguerite. For twenty-seven years she thrived on her work as an operating room nurse. Whether it was 2:00 A.M. or 2:00 P.M., organizing that operating room and assisting in those operations was her work, the patients were her patients, she could not conceive of herself doing anything that satisfied her more. Her self-image was built on the work.

When hospital policy required her to retire at age sixty-seven, the surgeons dedicated the hospital's new nurses' lounge to her. She found this gratifying, but there was a problem. Like Glen, she felt that she'd been put out to pasture. She was still powerfully healthy and wanted and needed to care for people. That was her work, it was a large part of her identity, and she was not done yet. No gold watch could compensate for the emptiness retirement caused her. She also misses the income.

The notion that someone can stop working after developing her expertise so fully and enjoy the change is naive. It is the product of minds that consider work a burden. People who think this way usually fit into one of three categories: they have never worked, they have spent too much time doing work that does not fit them, or they want to sell you retirement services.

Aim to Live Large

How much are you banking on the myth of retirement? Are you compromising today to finance a tomorrow that may never dawn and that you wouldn't enjoy even if it did? How do you see your work? Compare times when you were doing work that made time fly with other moments. It's fun to take a cruise or play golf, but being lost in work that is rich in self-expression is a rarer form of living.

What can you and your partner do to avoid being disappointed by this myth? Aim to live large.

First, be aware of what constitutes a worthwhile life—connection with and contribution to others, the self-esteem that comes from developing your talent and supporting yourself, and the satisfaction of sharing these accomplishments with your partner.

Be aware that you need to save so you can be you, not so you can retire from life. This awareness will help you give yourselves permission to invest money in you, even if you have to take it out of savings, even if you have to take it out of a retirement account. You cannot fulfill your promise unless you finance it.

Next, instead of trying to live without working, plan to do work that will satisfy and last. Concentrate on being accomplished for as long as you are physically and intellectually capable in life. Instead of working at a job from which you know you must retire at age sixty-five, use your ingenuity to come up with work that can last in some form or other, good health willing, until you are eighty or eighty-five. Paint, consult, create—develop expertise at bringing your promise all the way to customers so that later in life you can continue to do this. Maybe you can share the wisdom you've accumulated by working with others in an advisory capacity. Glen, for example, is using some of the wealth and wisdom he accumulated while launching three successful start-ups to assist in the nurturing of two new firms. Perhaps you can develop a similar role for yourself.

And finally, from now on, think more deliberately when you look at those retirement advertisements. Practice having a more intentional thought pattern. Consciously see retirement for the financial fairy tale that it is.

Prudential recently ran an ad in *Harper's* touting its retirement services. It read, "When I retire? I want to collect American folk art. I'm even thinking of buying a bed-and-breakfast to show it off in. Do you think we better get more aggressive?"

The answer is yes, you'd better. Not by postponing life several decades and engaging in stock market gymnastics in the interim, however, but rather by starting to live life today.

MYTH #2: NEGOTIATE TO WIN OR YOU'LL LOSE

Ray and his wife were selling a $240,000 house in California and buying a $260,000 home in Colorado, where he had just started a new job. His wife was still at their California home with their three girls, ages three, five, and seven, packing up and preparing to move.

One week before close of escrow, which was scheduled for the second week in December, the buyers presented Ray with a termite report calling for $225 in repairs on the California house. Under the terms of the sales agreement, Ray was required to make these repairs to complete the sale. Upset at having to absorb this cost, Ray declared that the termite company was a fraud and told everyone connected with the deals in both states that if he had to pay for those repairs, both deals were off.

Unpack the California house, back out of the Colorado house, find a new buyer, find another new home, reschedule the movers, and meanwhile split the family apart for most of the Christmas season—Ray was ready to bring all these burdens on himself and his family over $225.

For three days Ray's wife and daughters lived with the half-packed boxes, the prospect of having to reconstruct their move, and the message that their life together was worth less than $225. Resentfully, he finally gave in, paid for the repairs, and allowed the deals to close.

Ray's attempt to play the heavy hitter and try to win the negotiation is hardly unusual. Money and winning are deeply mixed together in our culture. Sales experts write books about how to negotiate and win. Management experts write articles about how to "beat the competition." Employers frequently demand a "team approach" on the job. Many companies are willing to pay $20,000 to $45,000 so the employees can hear what Pat Riley, Rick Pitino, Lou Holtz, or other professional sports coaches have to say about improving net operating income and meeting sales goals.

Yet as Ray's case demonstrates, when you try to play the heavy hitter, you are often unaware that the people closest to you are the ones who take the beating.

What people like Ray don't understand is that there is no such thing as winning a negotiation, because there is no winning in life. No trophy. No blue ribbon. No ticker-tape parade. You cannot win life. A negotiation contains only the opportunity that is present in every moment of life—the opportunity to fulfill your own promise or impede your own progress.

Trying to win a negotiation is detrimental to your interests in several respects. When you try to win, you put yourself in an adversarial posture with respect to those you negotiate with, and this never helps in moving a transaction or a piece of work to completion.

An emphasis on winning also puts arbitrary pressure on you and your partner to produce a specific outcome—sell the house for no less than $240,000, earn no less than $45,500 this year—when in fact many elements of the situation are well beyond your control.

Furthermore, you can never tell when you've won, because life comes with no referees, no time clock, and no scoreboard. Since I successfully negotiated for $500 extra, the thinking goes, does that mean that I probably could have gotten $1,000? And if a regular effort would have yielded $1,000 extra, would a polished, well-calculated effort have won me $2,000? Oh, no, was I really taken in this deal? Did I leave money on the table? There's no unbiased, reliable way to tell whether you won or lost.

Consuming yourself with winning negotiations also narrows your vision so much that you cannot conceive of alternatives. You never realize that you have other methods at your disposal for obtaining what you seek.

A More Enlightened Tack

Are you trying to win your real estate negotiations? The salary negotiations with the people you hire, or with those who hire you? To what extent do you feel that this stance is interrupting your life?

What do you get when you win? How do you feel when you lose? Has winning got you so twisted around that you want to win your negotiations, and yet you also want the other party to be able to win, too?

Since trying to win a negotiation typically turns it into a mess, consider instead a series of more enlightened tacks.

First, be aware that your negotiation, whether it involves a $200 stereo, a $2,000 raise, or a $200,000 real estate investment, is not a contrived situation, like a game of football or a round of golf. This negotiation is part of life. The question is whether you help yourself flourish in this moment. Either you accomplish this or you impede your own evolution. There will be no awards banquet.

Next, return to the basic steps for being articulate about money. These were outlined in Chapter 2: set up the connection, express yourself, and navigate with soul. These basic steps apply just as much to your negotiations with others as they do to your money discussions with your partner, with one modification: you obviously are not going to have a soul-to-soul discussion with the person who's buying your house. Instead, you'll have that discussion with yourself and with your partner, and you'll navigate based on the life you are trying to create.

This is where Ray failed. He never considered, either with his wife or on his own, how the terms of the negotiation were helping him and Debbie with the life they were trying to create. He would have profited from taking a look at some of these issues:

- How does this negotiation affect the work we do, the relationship we want, our spiritual lives, and the way we want to raise our children?
- Is this person I'm negotiating with a good one to go through this experience with? Does she have the financial horsepower to do what she promises so that the dealings will not bog down in problems that will distract me from my work and my life?
- Is she a master of disaster, or can she deliver what she promises without incident?

Had he asked these questions, Ray would have seen that, given the complexity of their plans, $225 was hardly a showstopping amount.

As you articulate your negotiating position, be deliberate. If you are negotiating for a house or for work, think about the issues overnight. Don't try to force a conclusion too quickly. Ask for what you want without pushing. Remember that your responsibility is to express your own position, not to worry about whether the person on the other side is winning. Take the time to outline your position in a letter or some other written document. This is an excellent way to collect your thoughts and to convey them in an unthreatening yet compelling fashion.

Finally, remember there are no magic words to make a person do what you want to do. There are ways to achieve your aims, however, if you can expand the field of negotiation. Sometimes, for example, fortune smiles on you and you have more than one buyer for your house or more than one bidder for your services. This brings an ease to your negotiating that is often quite compelling. If this doesn't work out, you think, my partner and I can work on the next candidate.

What about when there doesn't seem to be another potential buyer or employer? This is where being accomplished can play a pivotal role in your life. When you are focused on doing work that fits you, cultivating your talent, and bringing your promise to people, you have the capacity to develop other options for yourself. You have other ways to bring the funds you require in the door, so the specific terms of any single negotiation—whether it's for a job, a house, or a beach blanket—are not so desperately critical to you.

When you are accomplished, aware, deliberate, and articulate, you can achieve a sense of detachment from negotiations. This detachment will always make negotiating easier and will usually make it more profitable.

MYTH #3: MONEY IS EVIL, AND SO ARE THOSE WHO HAVE IT

Recently I represented Jim and Darlene in their effort to purchase a home. They had met the seller and liked him, and they felt that they would be able to come to a meeting of the minds. Though Jim and Darlene wanted the home very much, they were unsuccessful in their negotiations because they could not meet the seller's price. They could afford to pay only $200,000 for the property, and the seller was quite convinced that the property was worth at least $240,000.

The moment the stalemate became apparent, my clients had a surprising reaction. Darlene's first words were "I guess Mr. Parks isn't as altruistic as we thought."

I was surprised to hear her say that the transaction turned on Mr. Parks's altruism. I looked at her to see if she was joking, but the tightness of her jaw and the disgust on her face indicated that she was quite serious. She was convinced that she was locked in a struggle with one of Satan's poker buddies just because she couldn't have what she wanted.

The unvarnished truth was that Jim and Darlene did not have enough cash to afford a $240,000 house. To earn more, they would have had to change the work they did so they would be more valuable to people and thus command a higher income. This would have required some self-examination, some self-expression, and some effort. Alternatively, they could have constructed a life without a $240,000 house. Instead, they seemed more comfortable with frustration, resentment, and ill will.

"Money and those who possess it are evil"—you will not hear people say these exact words, nor will you find them in print, but the basic concept has a wide and active circulation nonetheless. It tends to be disseminated by people who are unaware of money's complete yield, people who don't know how to find work that fits them, and people who misinterpret the Bible.

For the record, the notion is entirely unfounded. Dollar bills are not evil. Take a stack of twenties, put them on the dining room table, and watch. They cause no mischief. This is not surprising. The Bible, at 1 Timothy 6:10, says, *"The love of money is the root of all evil"* (italics mine). Infatuation with the commodity is cited as the problem. The dollar bills themselves are in the clear.

By and large, people who ask for what they want when they sell their houses, offer employment, or propose an investment are not evil, either. If they are lying to you to achieve their ends, they will probably make poor dinner guests, but for the most part, people like Mr. Parks are simply taking a stand they think works for their life.

Despite its lack of substance, this myth is easy to slip into because it offers a simple explanation for why you cannot negotiate successfully for a house or command as much income for your work as you would like—because those people are horrible human beings.

This sort of thinking tends to make you feel better—self-righteously superior—for a moment. Over time, however, it keeps you and your partner from taking responsibility for your own life. You start to feel victimized a lot. Meanwhile the resentment, frustration, and ill will accumulate, and the life that you once thought you would have together seems farther and farther away.

A lot of problems evaporate, however, if you simply work this myth out of your thinking.

See No Evil

Consider the following questions:

• Are you spending energy blaming others for your perceived financial misfortunes when you could be using that energy to find work that fits you?

• Do you refrain from asking for what you want under the guise of being virtuous, and then resent those who articulate their desires and use money to realize them?

• Are you afraid to allow your children to work, for fear that they will somehow be corrupted?

• Does it seem to you that you have to deal with a lot of crooks?

• When money is the topic, do you often find yourself being righteous?

• Do you find yourself saying, "That's the business world and you're sure to be screwed, so don't bother"?

If the number of affirmative responses you scored leaves you feeling somewhat self-conscious, you could profit from a more rigorous application of money's fundamentals.

First, don't be quick to assume that people with a lot of money, or people who do not agree to your every financial proposal, are seriously flawed individuals. The point here isn't to categorize them as saints, either. The point is not to bother looking for evil.

When you find yourself making a judgment about a person's morality, retreat from it. You and your partner don't have time for this; you have more important things to do. Focus instead on being aware of whether the transaction you are trying to arrange can actually come together. Is the seller really motivated and ready to sell, or is he a master of disaster? Do you really have the funds and the motivation to complete the purchase?

Can the person who wants to hire you really deliver the work and the pay she promises? Does the work she proposes really fit you, and are you appropriately motivated to do it? These sorts of questions will give you the information that you and your partner need to move your lives forward.

Next, practice being articulate about money, especially in asking for what you want. Pay close attention to the practice of expressing yourself. You need not be righteous in your requests. Simply make them. You may be surprised at how willing people are to accommodate you.

Finally, put your time and energy into becoming accomplished instead of concerning yourselves with the exact extent to which someone else is in league with the Prince of Darkness. Find work that fits you and do that. The downside of this shift is that it will require that you relinquish the notion that one must make deals with the devil to succeed. The upside is that it will yield a much more fruitful life together.

Myth #4: Job Security Will Solve My Problems

Lisa and her husband decided to separate. In discussing their decision, she pointed out that, within six months, both of them had been laid off from "dead-end jobs with no security."

Property management had never appealed to Lisa in any important way, yet that was how she had earned an income for the previous three years, so that was where she looked for a new job. After some months she landed one that paid almost as much as her prior position. The new firm's prospects were questionable, but she considered that a sign of the times.

Lack of job security is not the sole reason Lisa and her husband grew apart. Looking for security and not finding it, however, hardly brought good sentiments into their home on a nightly basis. By not pursuing work that was more meaningful to them, they had one less bright spot in their day to talk about together, one less piece of themselves that they knew well and could reveal to the other. At dinner each night, instead of a passion to share, they each had a dispiriting story to tell.

How do you and your partner keep from starting down this road? One key is to make quite sure that you are not searching for job security. Plenty of articles are being published in financial magazines and newspapers declaring that job security has evaporated forever. Other articles and authors maintain that there are new rules for obtaining this most elusive commodity. The truth is that job security has never existed and it never will.

To the extent that people working in decades prior to this one felt that they had job security, theirs was a false sense of security, akin to walking on ice ignorant of the fact that ice can melt or crack.

Perhaps the companies these people worked for were enjoying unprecedented growth in sales and expansion of market share. This growth may have enabled these companies to pay people for months and years without interruption. The unthinking worker may have inferred from this good fortune that some sort of unwritten employment contract existed between him and his employer. In fact, this was never the case. It has always been the responsibility of a person proposing to work to demonstrate that the work will be valuable to those who receive it. It has always been the responsibility of one who works to be accomplished.

If you and your partner ignore this truth and attempt to rely on the myth of job security for your income, the price you pay will usually be steep. The typical problem is that in the event your employer no longer needs your services, you don't have your talents in shape, you don't have a very evolved vision of what you can do, and your sense of how to present people with a compelling offer is undeveloped. Like Lisa, you are put in a position where you must react to events instead of initiating them, and you must settle for less income than you are capable of earning and less satisfaction than you seek.

In such instances it's common to feel anxious and to sense that life is not working out. None of this has an uplifting influence on a relationship.

If you can make sure not to depend on a myth for your

income, however, you can take a lot of the downward pressure off your life.

Security Is a Muscle

Shortly after graduating from college, while he was a draftsman for an architect, Michael, the sports photographer profiled in Chapter 5, moonlighted for companies that needed brochure pictures of their products. He then shifted into doing product shots full-time and handled the occasional sports assignment on the side. Next, he ventured full-time into sports assignments and started his stock photo library on the side. Today, his primary work is keeping the stock photo library up to date while he does the occasional assignment.

Today, Michael possesses a sense of security about his income because he built it like a muscle by repeatedly taking the risks that enabled him to become more accomplished. You and your partner can build the same sense of security by committing yourselves to work that fits you.

Consider some questions:

• Are you relying on someone else to provide you with job security?

• Have the last two job changes you have made been your idea, or were you forced to make them because of your employer's decisions?

• Do you know what work you want to be doing in five years?

• If your current job ends, how will you make progress toward this aim?

• Do you have some sense that you are lunging from job to job?

- Are you working off a vision for yourself that is more than a decade old?

If the answers to these questions make you a bit uncomfortable, chances are you are relying on job security more than is wise and you need to devote yourself to becoming accomplished. What is your promise? Are you leaning on your talent and developing connections with customers? You can cultivate your talent while working for yourself, and you can also refine it while working for someone else. Your vision of who you are and what you can do simply has to be in sync with the work performed by the company that employs you. If it is not, you simply need to find different employment.

Security with respect to your income does not lie in years of service to a firm or in external economic conditions like steady demand for your company's products. The type of security you seek is a function of having a track record of making connections of value with the people you serve. Ultimately, it's an inside job.

MYTH #5: THE PARTNER WHO EARNS MORE KNOWS MORE

Thomas, who started an Internet company and sold it to a large Silicon Valley software firm for an enormous sum of money, did not know what to do. He and his wife, Melissa, were negotiating the purchase of a million-dollar house. They had been looking for almost a year. The sellers of this particular property had not been helpful during the inspection of the premises, and the buyers had reservations about the quality of the workmanship on the house's extensive renovations. The time to go forward or to drop the deal, however, had arrived.

Thomas and I discussed the problem. I pointed out their options as I saw them. Thomas thought for a moment, then asked, "What would you do?"

Now it was my turn to think. I remembered when Nancy and I had purchased our house. I had looked at a lot of houses and was sort of housed out by the time we found one we liked, so I asked Nancy what she wanted to do. She said make an offer, she named the price, we bought the house, and we have lived there happily ever since.

Returning to Thomas, I told him to ask Melissa—who, unlike him, had never sold a company she'd started for an enormous sum of money—what to do. Thomas put down the phone to go find his wife. A minute later he returned. "She says buy the house already." End of discussion. The deal closes. Happiness ensues.

There are two dangers in buying into the myth that the partner who earns more knows more. First, if you have just one person making most of the important decisions, that person is not necessarily the most qualified. Thomas had slogged through much of the tough negotiating with the seller on his deal. Even though he had brought home far bigger paychecks than Melissa, she was the one with the more detached perspective on this particular transaction. They both knew they needed to move on with life, but Melissa was able to declare it more emphatically because of her position.

The other danger in letting this earner-is-smarter myth creep into your relationship is that one person can become so accustomed to making the tough financial decisions that he will start making some of the others as well. Instead of just deciding when to buy a house, for example, he may call the shots on when to fix it, when to wash the car, when to buy groceries, and what his partner should wear. This is not necessarily a mean-spirited habit. It's just a case of one person being in the habit of doing the heavy thinking, and it is an expansion of power that your relationship can do without.

Refusing to succumb to the myth, however, can yield a substantial and enduring benefit: over time you will build a real partnership of equals. Your life will reflect your joint vision. It will be the product of your collective wisdom.

Share the Creative Control

Are you quietly buying into this myth? In a subtle way are you running the show or relinquishing control? Are you undercutting your partner's ability to contribute to your relationship, to do work that moves her, and to become the person she is capable of being by silently signaling that she is not qualified to make important decisions?

Two fundamentals in particular can help you keep this myth from creeping into your life together.

First, practice some awareness about how you handle your finances. Whether you are earning the higher or the lower amount, understand that the income differential could be temporary. No need to feel superior because you earn more. No need to feel inferior because you earn less. Who knows what will happen in the coming decade? If your partner starts a comic strip that becomes a multimillion-dollar source of income, you will not want to be silenced all of a sudden for past sins. Act as if you both have enormous income potential as well as correspondingly valuable opinions.

Second, speak up. If you are earning more, make sure that from time to time you ask your partner, "What do you think we should do?" and then do exactly that. Do it for the small issues such as who should drive to the frozen yogurt shop. Do it for larger issues such as what kind of car you should buy.

If you are earning less and not receiving enough opportunities to influence events, make sure that on occasion you say, "I want to do [whatever]." Then gently but firmly help your partner see that you are insisting on it. Make some small requests, and make some larger ones, too, until you feel the balance of creative control coming back into alignment.

Remember there is nothing here to win, nothing to compete over. A marrying of the spirit requires two parties. A life together is a co-creation, and you cannot collaborate unless you both participate.

THE FINAL WORD ON THE MYTHS

One last word about the myths of money: watch what you say very closely and do not let these myths seep into conversations in which you and your partner take part.

Excuse yourself from the discussions at the office about where to retire to. When a car salesman says, "I guess I'll have to speak to your husband," let him know that the decision-maker is standing right in front of him.

Steer the conversation elsewhere if your tennis partner starts chatting away about how Donald Trump, just because he's rich, must be aligned with Ming the Merciless. When your sister says that she worries about your partner because his company is having troubles, tell her she need not worry because your partner is so talented.

When you go with the flow of these myth-laden exchanges,

you give these myths life. This sort of behavior cements in your mind the very fabrications you need to avoid.

The truth is that money myths, along with the financial customs discussed in Chapter 6, are woven deep into our culture and will not disappear anytime soon. A lot of people live their lives according to these myths and customs, even though they are not necessarily pleased with the results. Accordingly, you and your partner may not find a lot of people to pattern yourselves after. This is no reason to lower your sights and settle for less in your life.

Money's fundamentals—not the customs and myths of personal finance that you may read and hear about so endlessly— are the practices that will carry you to money's multifaceted richness. You and your partner must take care to make these practices a habit, for you will need them more than ever when you hit high-stress money times.

PRACTICE

1. Make a list of the things you want to do when you retire. How could you make the experience of those years richer? Think about what you wanted to do in life before you learned about retirement. Consider skipping the part where you spend decades struggling to earn the funds to finance your ideas. Buy yourself a cake instead, declare yourself retired, and as you enjoy the cake, list seven ways you could finance the activities you thought would have to wait until you turned sixty-five.

2. Write down what you want to be known for at the end of your life. Are you working on that now? How could you step up the pace?

3. Think of a time when you tried to win a negotiation and really blew the situation for yourself.

4. Write a paragraph about your experience with the notion that money is evil.

5. Name five ways you could earn income if work you are currently doing suddenly evaporated.

6. How do you assess the way in which you and your partner share creative control? Does any one particular issue cause an imbalance? Propose an adjustment to your partner.

7. Do one of the following activities:

• Let your spouse drive the good car for a week while you take the clunker.

• Let your partner choose the dinner spot or picnic menu on your next date.

• Let your partner set the plans for your weekend.

• Ask your spouse to tell you over dinner what she wants your life together to look like. Listen. Instead of responding in kind, discuss a way to take one step toward realizing part of her vision.

The following week, switch roles with your partner.

Circuit Training

1. Arrange for some time off to be together in the next two months.

2. If you have a television in the bedroom, dining room, kitchen, or living room, move it to a room where you spend less time.

3. Practice being on time.

4. Set up one day in the next couple of weeks in which you extend your workout, whether it's walking, swimming, running, or yoga, by an extra ten to twenty-five minutes.

8 High-Stress Money Times

Seizing the Opportunity
Within the Crisis

Casey made $180,000 on a real estate deal one year. He and his wife paid off their bills, then bought themselves a beach cottage, a new BMW, and clothes clothes clothes. Before the year was out, they were borrowing money from Laura's mother again.

The next year Casey made another big deal, this one for $150,000. The couple paid off some of their bills, then started an addition to their house, took two Hawaiian vacations, and bought clothes clothes diamonds. Once again they needed a loan to make it through the year.

The following year Casey's big deal never materialized and he earned little income. By year's end he and Laura were so strapped for cash they had to sell the beach cottage.

The ecstasy and anxiety of their chase-the-big-deal, hit-the-mall, money-is-no-object, whoa-we-need-a-loan roller-coaster ride were also taking a toll. Casey, fancying himself a big hitter having a bad year, began bad-mouthing his firm about how poorly they were treating him. Laura kept telling him he should find a job with greater income potential. He typically responded by asking her what she could do to earn six-figure paychecks. Their first priority for the new year was to decide whether they needed to declare bankruptcy.

There are two times in particular when negotiating a marriage of true minds is an especially arduous task: when you take possession of a large chunk of funds, and when you face your idea of financial bad news. Because of the high anxiety attached to each of these situations, your first impulse may be to think that the fundamentals do not apply. In fact, whether you are dealing with a jackpot or a disaster, methodically practicing the fundamentals remains the key to being able to thrive. Sometimes it is even the key to your very survival.

DEALING WITH A JACKPOT

Years ago a young man who was a good college basketball player was the second choice in the National Basketball Association draft. With this one stroke of good fortune, fame and popularity burst into his life. With the contract he was expected to sign in the ensuing weeks, he would become a millionaire.

The day after the draft, the young man traveled to Boston to be welcomed by officials from his new team. That night he returned to his dormitory and celebrated his fortune with friends. Around midnight he ate some crab legs. Later he took some cocaine, and it killed him.

Reacting to the depth of this tragedy, one can identify a number of truths. One of them is this: if there had been no chance-of-a-lifetime selection in the NBA draft, the young man would probably still be alive. The fact is that sudden success and a sudden increase in wealth can be extremely difficult to deal with, and occasionally it can be lethal.

You and your partner need to learn to deal with sudden large bursts of income because they are part of life and they can bankrupt your finances, your relationship, and your soul if you handle them poorly. Your work may pay off to an extent you cannot possibly imagine as you sit there today. You may inherit a huge sum or earn a staggering profit because of a timely investment. To maximize the portion of the funds you hang on to, minimize the upset they cause you, and ensure that you don't lose your partner in the course of navigating this challenge, use money's fundamentals as handrails to take the following methodical steps.

Be Aware

The difficulty with sudden affluence is rooted in our reaction to it: we think life should be different when a huge chunk of cash shows up, and yet the cash never changes life in any important way.

If you were at odds with your spouse before the bonanza, you will probably still be at odds with him after its appearance. If you were unsure about what work to do in life prior to the jackpot, you will most likely still have questions about that work after your trip to the bank.

If you were counting on life being different and better because of all the dollars, however, or even just wondering whether they would make a difference, the reality that little of meaning has changed can be depressing. It can feel like a crisis. Life should be different, but it's not. Something must be terribly wrong. This feeling can prompt you to make exactly the wrong move: you try to do something with the dollars to make your fairy-tale expectation come to life.

You buy a pallet of French champagne, a Ferrari, a boat, or a Winnebago. You purchase a house, a second house, or a trip around the world. None of these purchases are bad, but they do not help you flourish in life. They don't bolster your connection with others, your relationship with your partner, or your self-esteem in any lasting way. If you keep trying to make champagne, Ferraris, houses, or plane tickets perform these feats, you typically squander your windfall, and you also feel empty because you are not engaged in activities that actually would enhance your connection to others, your relationship, or your self-esteem.

You thus lose track of yourself in the depressing gap you have created between expectation and reality. Adrift in this gap, you can easily blow your funds, your relationship, and your sense of who you are. If you are really unfortunate, like the young basketball player, you lose your life.

The best step, if you can manage it, is to be aware of the truth from the outset: the sudden arrival of wealth does not change anything essential to you. Intimacy with your partner, making good on your promise as a human being, connecting with others, supporting yourself—these are still your aims, because there is plenty of life left to live.

In the moment of seeing that wealth does not alter the essentials of your life, you transform the situation and recapture the opportunity that exists in every moment of every day: bringing forth your promise is still the main work of your life. Instead of being deeply disappointed that the dollars cannot change your life for the better and thus appear to be worthless, you can reclaim responsibility for working on your life.

With this single intellectual step, you transform the situation from crisis to opportunity, and you can grow instead of suffer. This one bit of consciousness also vastly improves your chances of hanging on to your wealth.

Be Deliberate

In practice, as you are holding your bank statement and attempting to fathom your staggering new bank balance, being fully conscious of the fact that it does not change the essentials of your life can be virtually impossible. It may take quite a while for this wisdom to emerge. While you wait, take a second step: slow down.

The day I earned that $225,000 commission, right after I checked my check 287 times on the way to the bank, I didn't know what to do with myself. What was appropriate—go drink some champagne? Grab some friends and go for champagne? It was about 2:00 P.M. when I deposited the check, and everyone I could think of was at work. I wound up going to Macy's, and after wandering around for a while, I bought myself a Ralph Lauren tie for $35.

The tie was a purple stripe, I remember, and it was not excruciatingly ugly, but purchasing it was a completely pointless act. At the time I owned about four dozen very elegant Zegna and Barbera ties that I had bought over the years. These ties folded into good-looking knots, hung nicely, and complemented my suits impeccably. The jackpot-day tie, by contrast, folded into a bulky, unattractive knot, jutted out from my collar with the grace of a two-by-four, and looked entirely out of place with my suits and sport coats. It hung in my closet unworn until I gave it to charity.

In retrospect, I see that I bought this tie while torn between expecting the dollars to change my life and realizing that they weren't going to. Fortunately, I felt sufficiently out of sorts that I sought fulfillment in a mere necktie and didn't try to buy a car, a stock portfolio, or a house.

This is what happens when you try to handle your dollars in

the wake of a jackpot. You make poor decisions because your judgment is understandably but undeniably out of whack and your good taste is out to lunch. You wind up with stuff. This stuff is typically useless, it usually can't be traded in for what you paid for it, and it constantly reminds you of an episode you would rather forget.

In the event you and your partner hit a jackpot, the temptation to make the dollars make a difference in your life will be huge. You may want to spend them on gifts for yourselves or your family, or you may decide to invest them to make them grow. Understand that your impulses are natural, that some of them may be good-hearted, but that, at the moment, your judgment is severely impaired.

Given that money decisions are so difficult, the best thing to do is to make as few as humanly possible. Pay off your debts, pay cash for your expenses, and put the rest of your windfall in the bank. Not the stock market—the bank. A good old-fashioned savings account. For how long? Leave it there until you catch a glimpse of your promise, so it will be available to help you finance work that fits you. This may mean it will sit there for a long time. Fine. When you sense what work you really want to do, and you look in the bank and see the funds, you will be extremely pleased with yourselves.

In the meantime, go visit your sister. Spend some time with your partner. Come to a full stop at stop signs. Get a lot of exercise and rest. Move slowly and purposefully in the hours, days, and months following your good fortune so that you recapture the equilibrium of your life. When in doubt about what to do, take a walk or a nap. By moving deliberately, you give your mind and your body the opportunity to catch up with the truth—that life goes on, good fortune notwithstanding.

Don't be surprised, in this time immediately following your

upgrade in financial status, to see how paltry the jackpot starts to look. Frequently, after taxes, commissions, lawyers' fees, and expenses, you don't have as much wealth as you thought you were going to have. Do not be alarmed into taking action. In the wake of collecting my big check, I went from being about $50,000 in debt to having no debts and twenty-two months of expenses in the bank. This seemed like a stunningly short reserve to me, but obviously my judgment was still out of kilter about how this deal would change my life. I thought several times about whether I should invest some of these funds in a high-performance stock or commodities portfolio so I could have some really big money, but fortunately I never followed up on those thoughts.

It can take a year or more to recover your perspective in the wake of a jackpot, so as you take your check to the bank, plan on moving slowly for a while.

Be Articulate

As Casey and Laura's story demonstrates, shopping together is not a way for the two of you to stay close. A little is fine, but more than that is exhausting. Instead of patrolling the mall together, talk to each other frequently during this period, and make sure you two connect.

How do you want to take care of yourselves physically and spiritually? What work do you each want to do to bring forth your promise? What activities are healthy and nourishing for your children and your families? What's good for your romance? Soul-to-soul discussions can help you navigate this unusual period in a way that will reaffirm and strengthen the life you two are creating together. These talks can keep you thinking in terms of how to articulate the life you two are capable of, help you avoid acting impulsively, and keep you from being distracted and consumed by stocks and cars and vacations and clothes.

Be Accomplished

Finally, use this opportunity to consider your work. What do you think you can do? What are you here for? How can you cultivate your talent? Play some tennis, buy some extra ballet tickets, and enjoy yourselves, but remember that retiring will not satisfy you.

Furthermore, recognize that what you have been doing for work, even if it produced the jackpot you now enjoy, may no longer suit you. After all, you have been there, done that, and gotten the T-shirt. Chances are good that your success has made you ready for bigger, deeper challenges. The funds you have acquired can finance work that fits you, and this is where they will yield their greatest return.

Remember, too, that this is an opportunity for both of you. If only one of you takes advantage of it, you risk growing into a lopsided relationship in which one of you is fulfilled and the other is unengaged, resentful, disheartened, or maybe all three.

WHAT IF WE INHERIT A PORTFOLIO OF SECURITIES OR REAL ESTATE? In the short run, do as little with it as possible. A loved one has just passed away, and you need to adjust to life without this person. Later in the year, or perhaps in the following year, when you have had time to look at what you are doing for a living, you may want to trade out of these assets into cash so that you can finance work that fits you. You need to take the right risk with your funds. For now, though, focus on the transition to life without your loved one.

As part of this deliberate approach to your inheritance, make sure you don't start squabbling with the other heirs about the size and division of the estate. I know one family in which the four children were out in the hospital hallway arguing with their stepmother over their father's will within minutes of his death. In the wake of their emotion-laden tirades, those five people don't speak to one another anymore.

Don't give in to the temptation to joust about the estate. Much later you'll realize that you really did not covet those dollars. If you fall into bickering over them, statements will be made that people can never take back, you will create permanent ill will, and you will put a sorry punctuation mark on the end of the life of someone who at one time meant a lot to you. All of this will distract and depress you for a long, long time. Be deliberate instead, and take the high road.

WHOSE ADVICE CAN WE TRUST? Steer clear of people who have an interest in your assets—that is, those who give advice on a commission basis or who will earn a substantial amount in hourly fees only if you engage in some elaborate transaction. Advisers who receive their compensation this way are not evil people. They simply cannot be counted upon to render a completely unbiased opinion.

I know a couple who inherited her grandmother's house at a time when the property was worth about $430,000. In the course of deciding what to do with this asset, they spoke with a securities broker and a real estate agent. The securities broker maintained that the stock market was poised for an upswing, while the property broker characterized the home market as unstable and recommended a quick sale. Despite this counsel, the couple decided to keep the house and rent it, which was relatively easy to do because of a tight rental market.

As it turned out, the stock market did in fact rise in 1996, but so did the local property market. By simply renting the house out, the couple earned rental income of $15,000 for the year plus approximately $40,000 in appreciation. They saved themselves the real estate, escrow, and stockbroker fees associated with selling the property and reinvesting the proceeds. They also saved themselves the months of hassle that this process would have entailed.

Doing as little as possible with an investment is often the best way to capitalize on it, but this remains a well-kept secret because few financial people receive compensation for telling you to move deliberately. If you and your partner are unsure about what course to take with your newfound net worth, find someone older and wiser to talk to, someone who does not have an interest in your assets and who has herself handled some sizable assets. Pay her for her time if that's appropriate. Deep inside, you two know what to do in order to bring your promise forth, and sometimes all you really need is another person of substance to assure you that your instincts are sound.

DEALING WITH DISASTER

I recently met two couples with pretty much the same story. In each case the husband had unexpectedly lost his job shortly after his wife had hired a new staff person, at considerable expense, to work at her firm.

Faced with financial peril, one husband joined his wife's firm while the other launched his own consulting firm. Today, both couples are thrilled with the turns their lives have taken. The couple working together cannot imagine living any other way. The consultant has regained his former income, his wife's firm is thriving, and he now even has time to work on a novel.

"For all the worry about what we were going to have to give

up," says Katherine, "I'm amazed at how much better our life is today." Buoyed by her experience, she urges people not to be disheartened by a sudden reversal of fortune. "There's no guarantee your story will turn out as well as ours did," she points out. "It might be better."

It's easy to say these people were lucky, but this undervalues the magnitude of their accomplishment. The truth is that each couple met with financial misfortune and used it to their advantage. How did they manage this maneuver?

It's important for you and your partner to know, because you will inevitably confront some form of financial unpleasantness at some point in your life. Your employer might cut your pay. One of you could lose your job. You could bounce a very important check.

You might need to come up with $15,000 to cover a medical or adoption expense on short notice. An investor might pull out of a deal you are arranging. You could inadvertently let an insurance policy expire.

To negotiate such events as well as these couples have, you and your partner need to take the following steps in careful fashion.

Understand the Mechanics of the Problem

A large part of the difficulty caused by sudden financial misfortune stems from our reaction to the bad news. Whether you have just bounced a check or just lost your job, the dynamics of the distress you feel are the same: your idea of how life was going to go, and how it was going to be paid for, has been shattered.

You expected to be able to pay your bills on time all the time, but you have just ended a call from the bank's vice president informing you that your account is overdrawn by $2,300. You expected to earn income at a certain establishment for years to come, and you have just found out that the company does not require your services beyond lunchtime. Such developments can depress and consume you and leave you feeling inadequate because your survival—your life as you know it—is threatened.

With your equilibrium reeling from the torque of these developments, you and your partner can easily attempt to make precisely the wrong move—to cling to your expectation of how life was going to unfold.

You continue to think that a life without a bounced check is the only genuine sign of fiscal responsibility, and you begin wondering if your slip foreshadows bankruptcy. You continue to try to be a contract negotiator for a defense contractor, even though demand for people who do this is virtually nonexistent. In these instances you cling to an expectation that cannot possibly be fulfilled, and thus peace and satisfaction are impossible to find. Instead you create anxiety for yourself. In that frame of mind, it's difficult to do anything constructive for yourself. Clinging to your expectation thus only makes the crisis grow.

The best step, if you can manage it, is to be aware from the outset that fiscal misfortune does not change anything essential to you. Intimacy with your partner, material support for your life together, a meaningful bond with the people you serve, making good on your promise as a human being—these are still your aims, and there is plenty of life left to live. What is different is the path you will take on your way to realizing those aims.

In the moment of seeing that you and your partner do not need life to unfold exactly according to your plan in order for you to flourish, you transform the situation. Instead of thinking that all is lost, you can let go of your expectation and keep doing the work of bringing forth your promise. Creating this intellectual space gives you room to envision a new way for events to unfold—a new way to be paid, a new way to pay your bills—that will take you where you want to go.

By reworking their spending, drawing on their savings, and imagining some different ways to be paid, Katherine and her husband continued to bring income in and to grow. You and your partner can do the same. In the moment you realize this, you transform the situation from crisis to opportunity, and you can move your life forward instead of anguishing over the past.

Keep Your Poise

When you are staring at a pile of bills and you don't have the money to pay them, or when you cannot figure out what to do with yourself at home because you've had an office to go to for the past sixteen years, achieving an advanced state of consciousness about your predicament can be an impossible task. That's okay. Give yourselves time. Meanwhile, it is extremely important that you both move very deliberately.

Adjusting to the reality of some financial trauma is a time when you can easily make some thoroughly horrible decisions. Whether you are driving, working, spending, or eating, your bounced check or lost job can dominate your thoughts. When you're distracted in this way, it's easy to burn yourself making breakfast, head the wrong way down a one-way street, or bark at your partner for not having dinner ready precisely at 6:30 as you had requested. Without fully realizing the consequences of your actions, you can break a knuckle punching a wall or yell at your two-year-old for dawdling while he climbs into his high chair.

To avoid compounding your problems in this manner, you must center yourself. Take care not to think too much about the future. Find the moment and try to live there. No one is demanding the house keys right at the moment. Take one minute at a time. Work on not going off the deep end and not letting your spirit break. The IRS will not take the house in the next minute. You will not become homeless in the next minute. Remind yourself how safe you are.

You must also be purposeful in a physical sense. Get some exercise. Eat sensibly. Get sufficient rest.

The large temptation at these stressful times is to try to do things even though you are plainly distracted. The results frequently only aggravate the situation. Cancel some meetings, go home early, or postpone a family gathering if you feel overwhelmed. Go easy. Move deliberately. Both of you.

Stick Together

One summer day while I was in college my father lost his job as credit manager at a large Boston hotel. He had worked there a number of years and liked it quite a bit; he was let go through no fault of his own when the corporation that owned the place hired a general manager who wanted to pick his own management staff.

At the time I was working as a counselor at a basketball camp. I remember my parents and my sister came over for the evening scrimmages, and then the four of us went out to a nearby hamburger place and my father told me what had gone on for him that day.

My parents were hardly rich, and I suspect this development

caused them more emotional ups and downs than they might have let Ann and me know. As we sat in the booth that evening, though, I did not sense that they were desperate or out of control, but instead that they were basically okay.

As we drank milk shakes, my father pointed out, "It's not like somebody died." We chuckled some about how the company had sent him to Harvard to take some sort of intelligence test before they hired him, and he pumped out one of the highest scores ever. Good guy to let go. Shrewd management on their part.

I remember feeling close to my parents and sister and also feeling some sense in the air that we would overcome this setback.

There were bumps in the financial road for my parents in the wake of Dad losing that job, but ultimately the path smoothed out. My mother continued to thrive on her job as a nurse at a local hospital. My father eventually started his own insurance inspection firm. This enabled him to eliminate the 120-mile daily drive to Boston and back, and to work for himself. Today, at seventy-five, he still works for himself. He swims five times a week, still runs his own firm, serves as the city's fire commissioner, and feels fortunate that he isn't sitting around wondering what to do with himself.

By sticking together, my folks gave themselves a base from which to weather the loss of my father's job. Katherine and her husband did the same, and sticking together will also be crucial to you and your partner if you face a similar storm.

If you two experience this sort of setback, make a point of being together, and follow the steps for being articulate with particular care. Set up the exchanges politely. Express yourselves. Make sure to listen to each other. Don't fall into bickering, blaming, or being uncommunicative.

Most of all, navigate with soul. Remind each other of all that is good with you: your health, your children, your faith in each other, and your love for each other. How can you take care of your health and each other? What work do you each want to do? Acknowledge your fears, but remember to articulate your hopes as well. You are not bad people. Financial unpleasantness happens. Life is not over. Not at all. Use your relationship as a safe harbor, a place from which to rebuild.

Go to Work

The fourth part of navigating a financial crisis is to go to work. Concern yourselves here with two particular tasks.

First, there is the issue that is causing the disruption in your life—the bounced check, the $15,000 that is due the IRS in three weeks, the impending loss of income. You need to deal with this issue. Katherine and her husband needed to cut expenses. My parents needed to renegotiate a loan. You may have to set up a payment plan with the IRS, take some funds out of an IRA, or take a job that is definitely not your first choice but that will enable you to pay the bills. Whatever the case, you and your partner need to cast aside any notion that you are bad or inept, and simply administrate your finances.

Second, devote yourselves to work that fits you. You may already be engaged full-time in such work, or you may just be starting out on a moonlighting or volunteer basis. Whatever the case, apply yourselves to becoming accomplished. You will both profit from focusing on this work because you can find peace in work that means a lot to you, and because ultimately this work will be the way you can bring a hefty chunk of cash into your life.

Instead of letting her new marketing person go and thus compromising her work, Katherine kept cultivating her talent. Her work and her husband's consulting and writing have replenished their reserves, brought them enough extra cash to resume taking vacations, and created bright prospects for their future. Their work also provided them each with a refuge from the anxiety caused by their setback.

Whether you have bounced a check or lost your job, send yourselves to work. It is a natural way to break out of the habit of creating anxiety, and the best way to put yourself in position to avoid having your fiscal problems recur.

Weathering the Storm

What will life look like as you implement money's fundamentals in dealing with a disaster?

Assume it is two-thirty on a sunny Monday afternoon in July and you are experiencing turbulence. Every time your phone rings you think it's the bank calling about the mortgage payment that was due last Thursday. You have just finished a very sharp conversation with your partner about whether this month's preschool tuition check should come out of his account or yours. Earlier today your boss ordered you to leave for Houston and Modesto tomorrow to calm customers who are angry about the company's troubled software programs. Assume, too, that amid all these demands, you and your partner aspire to a marriage of true minds. What do you do?

Sit up straight in your chair and take a deep breath. Remind yourself that you are okay.

Call your partner back and connect with him. Talk to him, and listen to him. Promise each other you will continue this connection when you get home later today.

Next, spend a prescribed amount of time—say, thirty minutes—dealing with the mortgage and cash flow problems. Don't try to solve them once and for all in one sitting. Call the bank. Talk to the lending officer. Be polite and be open. Apologize for being late. Tell him about what you are trying to create with your work and how you see your work paying off. Tell him about your partner's work as well, and let him know you will call by Friday with a plan for making the payment.

Then put your imagination to work. Spend some time coming up with ways to solve the problem. Savings? Borrow? What about that series of photographs you've been working on—is it time to see if you can sell it to a calendar publisher? Perhaps you need to consider refinancing. Don't press yourself for the final answer now. Just consider your options. You have more than you might suspect. Then shift to doing what you must to finish your day on the job, and get some exercise if you can.

When you arrive home, connect with your partner. Discuss the finances to the extent you need to, but start to shift the primary focus to work that fits—for both of you. Perhaps you already know what it is. Perhaps your partner knows but you need to catch a glimpse of your promise. How can you cultivate your talent? Wherever you are in that process, start logging some time there.

This is a marriage of true minds, after all. The idea is for the two of you to flourish and also to connect in a deep and meaningful way, circumstances notwithstanding. Admit no impediments. Concentrate on putting together a string of days like this, days in which the two of you stick together and attend to the problems at hand but also work on yourselves.

No one can predict exactly how you'll weather the storm, but there are signs that a promising future lies ahead.

PRACTICE

1. On becoming rich and having stuff: How could you cut down on stuff and have an easier and more fulfilling life? Could you live in a smaller house, drive fewer cars, sit on fewer boards of directors, do less shopping, dress more simply? Should you purchase some simplicity? Perhaps you need to sell a high-maintenance asset such as vintage car or a second house in snow country, even it that means taking a loss, or maybe you should engage someone else to clean your house and do the laundry.

2. On creating a trust of personal mettle for a child: Name your child's talents or those of a niece or nephew. If you are not sure, ask the child what his talents are, in his view. List five ways to help him cultivate those talents, and choose one to follow up on.

3. On facing what looks like disaster: How can you live in the moment, in which you are okay, more regularly? Perhaps you need to move more deliberately, take more deep breaths during the day, or shut the phone off after 6:00 P.M. and let it take messages. Maybe, when you feel yourself becoming tense about finance, you need to remind yourself that you have talent to bring forth and that now is not the time to lose your nerve.

4. Name five things you thought you needed in life but have learned you can flourish without.

Circuit Training

1. Revisit your soul-to-soul questions. What do you need to give up in order to live the life you want? Would those sacrifices be genuinely painful? List all the negatives of living that life. List all the positives.

2. How are your dates going? Make sure you are taking them regularly, and make sure they stay simple enough so that you and your partner can connect easily. Expensive dinners, trips to the opera, attendance at art openings—such affairs can be so elaborate that intimacy is not possible. If you are tense about finances and having trouble talking about anything but that, try watching a nonviolent movie.

3. Monitor your exercise regimen. Are you still working out regularly, economic fluctuations notwithstanding? Make sure not to overextend yourselves. You need to be fit but also fresh.

4. How are you doing in your efforts to catch a glimpse of your promise? What steps have you taken recently to cultivate your talents?

9 Negotiating a Marriage of the Spirit

Pete and Marlene went away for a three-day weekend with friends at a seaside resort. Pete was upset about the rumor at work on Thursday that his firm's bonuses that year were going to be very small, if indeed there were bonuses at all. Marlene urged him to relax, but to no avail. At one point he snapped, "How do you expect to pay for this trip?" In fact, during their marriage, Marlene had given up one job after another so they could make the moves that seemed best for Pete's career, and as a result her income was quite modest. Distracted by Pete's distress over their finances, they went home a day early.

Love took second place to finance in their life that weekend because Pete assumed that love had no cash value. This is not the enlightened viewpoint.

Love's worth is unknown. It's value is incalculable. This is much different from saying that love is worthless, and leaping from there to the conclusion that love and money don't mix. To negotiate a marriage of the spirit, you and your partner must let go of the notion that love and money are naturally incompatible pursuits. You cannot afford to let finance impede love, to live as if love is without cash value, because the truth is quite the opposite.

TRUEING UP YOUR MIND

Recall the experience of Simone and Jean Claude from Chapter 1. Starting Simone's firm presented the couple with great financial difficulties, but they did not give up on Simone's promise. By taking the steps necessary for her to fulfill that promise, they brought forth the handsomely profitable firm that she runs today.

If you examine their actions closely you will see that the couple relied heavily on money's fundamentals. They did not rush to the conclusion that she needed to take a job just for the income. When they discussed which direction to take in the difficult years, they navigated with soul. Simone kept her focus on being accomplished. Jean Claude consciously took a stake in his wife's work and stuck by it.

They hung on to their promise as human beings and let go of their financial fears, their preconceptions about how long success would be in coming, and their fixed ideas of what shape success would take. Money's fundamentals helped them choreograph a dance that paid off in the rich life they enjoy today.

Now return to the sonnet that precedes the Introduction:

Love's not Time's fool, though rosy lips and cheeks
Within his bending sickle's compass come;

The genuine lover, the sonnet implies, remains true to her vow to love her partner even as time passes and the shape and appearance of earthly matters like lips and cheeks run their natural course. Love is not fooled into being unsettled by these inevitable fluctuations and developments, but instead "looks on tempests," however large or small, "and is never shaken."

The marriage of true minds, we see, is a promise and a dance—a vow to love each other and a dance of letting go of trivial circumstances and staying true to one's bond. One value of love, then, is this: it reminds us of the key to using money wisely, for money, like love, is a promise and a dance.

When you and your partner forget this fact about money, your commitment to fulfilling your human promise crumbles and your life together suffers. Trying to speed through transactions, win negotiations, or earn a living without checking your messages—these moves will cost you cash. Signing on for the get-a-job-buy-a-house-save-for-retirement lifestyle, the Bermuda Triangle of personal finance, will in some important sense cost you your soul.

Perhaps most importantly, when you ignore money's fundamentals and let dollar bills consume your attention the way Pete did, you severely impede your ability to grow into a marriage of the spirit. Refusing to navigate with soul, allowing the fear of missing out to consume your attention, or failing to cultivate your talents and tailor your work to your relationship—in taking these actions, you essentially break the spirit of your vow to your partner. You settle for too little from yourself and fall short of your promise as a human being, so only a shadow of you shows up for the relationship. In addition, if you fail to take a stake in your partner, you most likely impair her chances of sharing a true mind with you.

The marrying of spirits you aspire to calls for you to commit all of each of you. You pledged yourselves to each other. No holding back. Everything you have. No more, but no less. The truth is that when you ignore money's fundamentals, you sabotage not only your finances but also this marrying of souls, and your union becomes a much smaller experience than it could be.

As the experience of Jean Claude and Simone demonstrates, by contrast, when you earn, invest, negotiate, and communicate about money with the understanding that money is a promise and a dance, finance does not impede your love. In this way love shows you the way to a life of great richness, one that includes plenty of cash.

Giving up the idea that money is evil, seeing opportunity in crisis, knowing all is never lost, negotiating and spending deliberately, and recognizing masters of disaster when they walk in the door—if you two are really serious about putting cash in the bank and keeping it, money's fundamentals are for you. Just because you want intangibles from money does not mean you must relegate yourselves to a life of poverty. Moreover, working your talents and investing in yourselves will point you toward a life that will nourish your sense of self-worth and your connection to the people you serve.

Best of all for the two of you, the fundamentals set you on a course that will enhance rather than undercut your efforts to achieve intimacy. You cultivate your talents and take a stake in her. She cultivates her talents and takes a stake in you. You cradle her dreams. She cradles yours. Regardless of the economics of the moment. In fulfilling your promise, you become richer, more evolved individuals. All of you shows up for the marrying.

By understanding that money takes a commitment to your human promise at every juncture, you and your partner each true up your mind and give yourselves a better chance to grow into a marriage of the spirit. Instead of living in financial fear of revealing yourselves, you set each other free to be who you are. In this way you fulfill not just the letter but the spirit of your vow to be true to each other.

A SIGNPOST OF PROMISE

Just because money's fundamentals are so basic does not mean money is always an easy task. The rich return on money we have discussed here, including the bond between the two of you, is negotiated in the literal sense of that word: it is *negotium,* which is to say, "not leisure." There are two people, two efforts, two sets of interests, perspectives, and desires to harmonize. Mingling money into this union will require work.

To listen to each other, to take a stake, to be deliberate, and to cultivate talent—these actions may not be your first choice when circumstances call for them. Taking these steps will thus sometimes require giving up your preference.

Working money myths out of your life can be difficult because it often entails creating space between you and the relative, friend, or adviser who planted the myth in your mind.

Freeing yourselves from financial custom can seem almost impossible, because Prudential, Merrill Lynch, and Century 21 spend millions each month on advertisements calculated to make you regard financial custom as your salvation in life.

To release yourselves from the struggle with money, become accomplished human beings, and forge a rich life together, you and your partner will have to choose your way past these obstacles. You two can indeed use money to flourish, but the task takes work, and at times you may struggle with the dance.

So there is a very simple question at the heart of the inescapable triangle formed by you, your partner, and money: which effort do you choose? The one in which you learn to set each other free or the one in which you live as shadows of yourselves? Every time you earn, spend, invest, negotiate, or communicate about money, you choose between these two options.

You may reasonably ask, "What guarantee do I have that a commitment to money's fundamentals will pay off for my partner and me as sweetly as it has for Simone and Jean Claude in terms of relationship, bankbook, and soul? How can my partner and I let go of our financial habits, as ineffective as they may be, with confidence that we will not perish?"

There is indeed much we do not understand about how our world works. Certainly you will receive nothing in writing about either money or love.

Yet consider the flow of human events that has brought you and your partner to this time and place together. What if the universe wants you to succeed? What if a second value of love is that your partner's vow is proof of your promise, acknowledgment from an independent corner of the universe that you are destined for greatness and worthy of success if you will only reveal yourself? What if, in pledging yourselves to each other, you have already shown yourselves capable of the essential dance you must master to keep your appointment with the universe?

We don't normally think of life this way, but just because we don't know about something with scientific certainty doesn't mean it isn't so. Perhaps the universe wants you to have self-esteem, connection to others, competence, ample material support, and a marriage of the spirit, and has equipped you perfectly to claim your birthright.

Perhaps, fueled by your spirit, guided by your vision, and armed with your talents, you are designed to make good on your promise and, in the same motion, to be faithful to your vow to your partner, to create a meaningful connection to those you serve, and to support yourself. The promise within you, the promise you exchanged with your partner, the promise at the heart of your work, and the promissory notes that help us support ourselves—perhaps these are all a part of the same promise, and the whole enterprise fits together perfectly.

You have been looking to get on a roll with your money. Loosen up. Let love lead. Perhaps the design, as far beyond our comprehension as it is, is that you let your talent do the work, and your promise is fulfilled in a way that is better than you could ever have imagined.

PRACTICE

1. Plan a relaxing weekend away from home.

2. Who supports both you and your partner in your life? Who needs to be edited out? How could you orchestrate life to spend more time with the people in the former group?

3. How is your exercise campaign going?

4. How could you be a bit better at helping your partner by cradling his dreams?

5. On one of your next dates, recall how you two fell in love and what sparked your initial attraction to each other. Figure out whether you crossed paths without knowing it before you met. List all of the incredible things that had to take place so you two could meet.

6. Give your partner a long, long hug. Look into her eyes, tell her you love her, and tell her why.

Notes

··

INTRODUCTION

9   Sherry Suib Cohen, "Don't Let Money Wreck Your Marriage," *Parade* magazine, March 12, 1995, p. 24.

4. THE PROFIT IN BEING DELIBERATE

137   "The Forbes 400," *Forbes,* October 14, 1996, pp. 108, 198.

5. THE FRUITS OF BEING ACCOMPLISHED

149   *Oxford English Dictionary,* 2d edition (1989), Vol. XVII, p. 580. See also *Webster's New 20th Century Dictionary of the English Language* (unabridged), 2d edition (1976), p. 1859.

153   Jonathan Curiel, "Spiders Just Can't Draw Flies," *San Francisco Chronicle,* February 7, 1996, p. D1; Associated Press, "IHL Spiders Appear Headed to Canada," *San Francisco Examiner,* April 11, 1997, p. B2.

6. QUIT THE FEAR-BASED LIFESTYLE

198   Department of Labor, Bureau of Labor Statistics, Consumer Price Index Hotline for the San Francisco Bay Area.

199   Ruthe Stein, "Another Chapter for Neil Simon," *San Francisco Chronicle,* October 11, 1996, p. C1.

203   Membership Report, National Association of Realtors, December 1996; U.S. Statistical Abstract (1996), p. 721.

204   Laura Castaneda, "How a Little Bit of Money Can Turn into a Nest Egg," *San Francisco Chronicle,* July 15, 1996, p. B1.

7. DISMANTLING FIVE MONEY MYTHS THAT CAN DRIVE YOU APART

218   Robert Reich, "Living Large in a Downsized World," *GQ,* May 1996, p. 163; Kenneth Howe, "Bay Residents Court Financial Disaster," *San Francisco Chronicle,* January 2, 1995, p. A1; Jackson National Life brochure; *The Charles Schwab Guide to Retirement Planning,* 1994, p. 2.

224   See, for example, Michael L. Tushman and Charles A. O'Reilly III, *Winning Through Innovation* (Cambridge, Mass.: Harvard Business School Press, 1997); Pat Riley, *The Winner Within* (New York: Berkeley, Trade, 1994); Guy Kawasaki, *How to Drive Your Competition Crazy* (New York: Hyperion, 1995); Robert H. Miles, *Corporate Comeback* (San Francisco; Jossey Books, 1997); and Robert Slater, *Get Better or Get Beaten* (Chicago: Richard H. Irwin, 1994); Donald Katz, "Words to Win By," *Sports Illustrated,* August 7, 1995, p. 68.

8. HIGH-STRESS MONEY TIMES

242   Ira Berkow, "The Bias Mystery," *New York Times,* June 22, 1986, p. s7; Associated Press, "Examiner Confirms Cocaine Killed Bias," *New York Times,* June 25, 1986.

9. NEGOTIATING A MARRIAGE OF THE SPIRIT

265   *Oxford English Dictionary,* Vol. X, p. 303. See also *Webster's New Collegiate Dictionary* (1973), p. 769.

Index

About the Author

....

William Francis Devine, Jr., is an attorney practicing in Palo Alto, California. He is president of the California Real Estate Clinic, a radically economical and healthy alternative to standard brokerage services. He is also editor of the national newsletter *Self-Worth Illustrated* and leads Women, Men & Money workshops throughout the country.

Devine has counseled individuals and couples from all income brackets as well as global financial institutions and Fortune 500 clients. He graduated from the Phillips Exeter Academy and received his B.A. from Dartmouth College. He earned his J.D. from Boston University School of Law, and is a member of the California Bar. He is also a former college basketball coach.

The author lives in Menlo Park, with Nancy, his wonderful, elegant, and eloquent wife, and Amanda, their slim, tall, fast, quick, smart, and pretty four-year-old daughter.

To share stories or ask questions, to find out about upcoming Women, Men & Money workshops, or to receive a copy of *Self-Worth Illustrated* or a list of available audio- and videotapes, please contact the author:

web site: http://www.wdevine.com
email: bill@wdevine.com
fax: 650-329-8985
mail: P. O. Box 60711
         Palo Alto, CA 94306-0711